Wednesdays at Eight

With God,
all Things are possible!.
Best Wishes,
Mary Mennut

Wednesdays at Eight

Everything You Always Wanted to Know About a Prayer Group, but Were Afraid to Ask

MARY MOUSSOT

iUniverse, Inc.
New York   Bloomington

Wednesdays at Eight
Everything You Always Wanted to Know About
a Prayer Group, but Were Afraid to Ask

iUniverse books may be ordered through booksellers or by contacting:

iUniverse
1663 Liberty Drive
Bloomington, IN 47403
www.iuniverse.com
1-800-Authors (1-800-288-4677)

ISBN: 978-1-4401-6182-7 (sc)
ISBN: 978-1-4401-6184-1 (dj)
ISBN: 978-1-4401-6183-4 (ebk)

Printed in the United States of America

iUniverse rev. date: 08/18/2009

Dedication

I dedicate this book to Nan Clark, who was instrumental in making this book a reality. Many years ago, Nan had the insight to suggest that I keep copies of the Inspired Thoughts and Prayerful Reflections which the Holy Spirit inspired me to share at our Wednesday night prayer meetings. If it were not for Nan, I would have most likely thrown my notes away. Through her encouragement, untold scraps of papers and folders of notes soon began to materialize into a book. Week after week, she patiently corrected grammar, spelling and punctuation. I owe Nan a debt of gratitude, because without her vision, her driving force encouraging me, and her complete support, I would never have been able to complete this task. I can honestly say that it is as much her book as it is mine. Thank you, dear friend.

Table of Contents

IV. Experience Your Own Prayer Meeting

V. Fifty-Two Inspired Thoughts and Prayerful Reflections

Foreword

God said, "Let there be light," and there was light.
(Genesis 1:3)

Thirty years ago on a Wednesday evening, in a remote section of the Bronx, a miracle occurred. A small band of Christians consisting of one priest, one nun, and a few lay people entered a church hall, formed a circle out of a few folding chairs, lit a candle, joined hands, and began to pray. That is how the St. Frances de Chantal Charismatic Prayer Group and <u>Wednesdays at Eight</u> was breathed into life. Thirty years later, each Wednesday night, the folding chairs are still opened, a candle is lit, and prayer begins.

Some of the faces have changed and the circle of chairs has grown. Many of the original members remain an integral part of the group. Throughout the years many others have joined us in prayer. Some came and prayed for years. Others came and prayed for a months. Still others came to pray just once or twice. One thing is certain. All who came, regardless of their length of stay, were touched by God in some way. And all who came truly believed: "For where two or three are gathered together in my name, there I am in the midst of them." (Matthew 18:20)

It is not by accident that the St. Frances de Chantal Prayer Group has endured. God is truly alive in each and every member, and one feels truly blessed to part of this wonderful miracle. Father Robert Grippo, one of the founding members and our Prayer Group's Spiritual Advisor, continually reminds us, "If it is of God, it will last; if not, it will fade away." (Acts 5:39) God has indeed shown us that it is his will that we come together every Wednesday at 8:00 PM by blessing us with thirty years of prayer and fellowship in the Lord.

Since becoming part of this prayer group, I have been especially blessed. After attending just a few meetings, I felt the Spirit inspiring me to use words to verbally share the experience of my own spiritual journey with others. The process by which this happens is always the same. I might be at home, in a store, reading a book, watching television, talking to a neighbor, or attending mass. Suddenly, a word or phrase that is spoken or a sentence that I read gives me a tiny seed of inspiration from which my reflection begins to develop. I have heard composers, writers and artists express that they experience this same phenomenon. Billy Joel, singer and composer noted that the inspiration for his song, "Scenes from an Italian Restaurant," came from a waiter who approached him with a wine list and casually asked, "A bottle of red, a bottle of white?" It resulted in one of Joel's greatest musical successes and best known works.

For me, the words begin to flow on a single word, phrase or sentence and my mind begins to race, thinking of what I must write down. I must put pen to paper immediately, because although God gave me the gift of gab, he did not give me a retentive memory. For this reason every table in my home has a pad and pen so that I can jot down my thoughts at a moment's notice.

Over the course of the days that follow, through encounters with people, books, newspapers, and the stuff of everyday life, my original idea receives confirmation over and over again, indicating that I am on the right track. I often refer to this as "manna from heaven." These confirmations spur further thoughts and much writing. I then compose a rough draft of the reflection and polish it until I feel it is worthy of sharing with the members of our prayer group. Once I have shared my reflection the most miraculous part of this process occurs. This is when others present testify that they too, received the same word, further confirmation of the word that I have just shared. The Spirit was speaking to each of us and all of us.

I am just one of the many vessels that God has chosen to spread his word and writing is one of the means God has called me to serve him. Writing and sharing words has truly become a spiritually fulfilling experience for me. I never feel such joy as when I say or write something that inspires and uplifts others spiritually!

But truly, we are all called to build up the Body of Christ. The Holy Spirit gifts each one of us in a unique way, and we must not be envious of the gifts given to others, but instead pray for discernment to recognize how the Lord wants us to use our own gifts. Open your heart to the promptings of the Spirit with complete trust that he will lead you to where you can best serve him. Share the gifts he has given, and you will feel the exuberance that comes from serving our Lord. When you feel the presence of the Holy Spirit in your life, you will realize he is using you in a special way. Then the words, "What you have received as a gift, you must give as a gift," (Matthew 10:8) take on new meaning. Saint Paul tells us, "There are different gifts, but the same Spirit. There are different kinds of service, but the same Lord. To one there is given through the Spirit, the message of wisdom; to another, the gift of healing; to another, miraculous powers; to another, prophecy; to another, speaking in different tongues. And it is the same one and Holy Spirit who gives all these gifts and powers, deciding on those which each of us should receive." (1 Corinthians 12:4-11)

The writing and sharing of my thoughts are gifts inspired by the Holy Spirit which have enriched my life immeasurably. This book is the result of the many times the Holy Spirit whispered in my ear and revealed to me some of the mysteries of life. These gifts did not come overnight but developed over many years from spending quiet time before our Lord in reflection and prayer. Harden not your heart when the Spirit speaks to you, but listen. It is the Holy Spirit who will light a fire within you, a fire that will not be quenched. Through the Holy Spirit you too, will be able to boldly proclaim the message of the gospel to those who have not heard it. As Saint Paul tells us, "Yet when I preach the gospel, I cannot boast, for I am compelled to preach. Woe to me if I do not preach the gospel. I would be utterly miserable." (1 Corinthians 9:15-16)

I owe a great debt of gratitude to the members of our prayer group who encouraged me to share my thoughts and I thank all of our gifted members for witnessing how the Holy Spirit has inspired them to build up the Body of Christ. The reflections that I have shared with them, I now humbly share with you so that they may inspire you too, to draw closer to him. Then there will be great cause for rejoicing since that is the purpose for which this book was written. Finally, if this book inspires the reader to seek out and become part of a prayer community or to start your own, the book and author have both achieved their ultimate purpose, because through you, our circle of chairs continues to grow, and the miracle continues. Amen!

Author's Note/Format of the Book

This book is intended not only for those already familiar with the setting and the structure of a Charismatic Prayer Meeting, but perhaps especially for those who are not and may have asked, "What actually is a prayer group?" It is meant to be a resource for those who would like to learn more about a prayer group and the type of prayer one would experience within a prayer meeting setting.

My purpose is to both inform and inspire readers. To inform, I have provided a brief history of the Charismatic Renewal Movement. You will then find a description of the structure of our prayer group, followed by the orderly sequence of prayer that occurs at every prayer meeting. To inspire, I have provided a compilation of Fifty-Two Inspired Thoughts and Prayerful Reflections motivated by the Spirit, that I have been moved to share at our weekly prayer meetings over the past twenty-five years. The book is formatted as follows:

Section I, **The Charismatic Renewal Movement** describes the movement that spurred the growth and spread of Charismatic Prayer Groups.

Section II, **Structure of a Prayer Group** will familiarize you with the configuration of a Prayer Group, the diverse ministries that make it up, and the purpose of each.

Section III, **Format of a Prayer Meeting** will introduce you to the orderly sequence of prayer, praise, song and meditation that takes place at each meeting.

Section IV, **Experience Your Own Prayer Meeting** is a step-by-step guide to help begin your own prayer time either individually or as a group. It has been formatted like a missal to allow you to easily follow the sequence of prayer from beginning to end, as though you were present with us at our meeting.

Section V, **Fifty Two Inspired Thoughts and Prayerful Reflections**, contains fifty-two sets of partnered prayers, one for each week of the year, to be used with your prayer missal.

Section VI, **Appendix**, contains additional information and resources to assist you in your prayer.

Finally, for those who might be interested in establishing their own prayer community, I hope that this book can serve as a sort of how-to manual to get you started. For those who have thought about seeking out and joining an existing prayer group, I pray that this book will spur you to do so. And for those that are less ambitious, my prayer is that this book will help you experience the joy of Charismatic prayer on an individual and personal basis, privately in the comfort of your own home.

I. The Charismatic Renewal Movement*

---

*   This section excerpted with permission, courtesy of Dr. J. Dominguez

1.

A Brief History

One cannot speak about Prayer Groups and Prayer Meetings without mentioning the Charismatic Renewal Movement. The Greek term "Charism" or "charisma" denotes any good gift that flows from God's benevolent love (*charis*) unto man, through the Holy Spirit. The plural is "Charisms" or "charismata". The word "Movement" differentiates it from an organization or a society. As a Movement, it has religious and lay leaders, directors of charismatic centers and events, but it doesn't have a hierarchy of president, secretary or treasurer, as any organization or society would have.

John the Baptist told his followers that the Messiah "will baptize you in the Holy Spirit and in fire." (Luke 3:16) In the Acts of the Apostles we see that the early church believed this and saw it come to pass, continually praying for the outpouring of the Spirit. Church history shows that this "Baptism in the Spirit" did not die with the Apostles, but continued in strength for centuries through the present day. The Catholic Charismatic Renewal is the latest of these expressions of Baptism in the Spirit and charismatic gifts.

The renewal of this experience of Baptism in the Spirit began in the Catholic Church in February of 1967 when a group of students on retreat at Duquesne University in Pittsburgh, Pennsylvania began praying for a fresh outpouring of Pentecost. Many of them had profound Baptism in the Spirit experiences that they shared with others in prayer. They began a renewed commitment to prayer, a personal relationship with Jesus, a yearning for more knowledge in their Catholic faith, a desire to answer the gospel call to bring the message of Jesus to others, and the use of the gifts and charisms of the Holy Spirit to bring this about.

By 1972 Leo Joseph Cardinal Suenens, Archbishop of Brussels, Belgium (1904-96), personally encountered the Charismatic Renewal during a visit to the United States. He was immediately taken by this encounter, because it appealed to his desire to see the Church flourish as in a new Pentecost through the work of the Holy Spirit. He became not only a spokesman but was appointed by Pope Paul VI as the movement's Vatican representative. In many ways Cardinal Suenens was an unlikely person to carry the banner for the Catholic Charismatic Renewal. Personally reserved, even shy, overly intellectual… as captured by Cardinal Danneels in his funeral homily, *"how could a cardinal with a face that did not show many emotions, with a straight and immobile stature, with a grave and steady voice, find himself at ease in the midst of a crowd that sang, danced, clapped hands and spoke in tongues?"*.

By 1990, in only 23 years, the movement had grown to include more than 100 million Catholics in over 238 nations. Many believe that this Charismatic Renewal is a direct result of Pope John XXIII's prayer at Vatican II, *"O Holy Spirit… pour forth the fullness of your gifts… Renew your wonders in this day as by a new Pentecost"*. There followed a wildfire movement of the Spirit so profound that it led to the spread of the movement throughout the United States and the world. This Renewal of "baptism in the Spirit" has "set on fire" for the Lord nine million Catholic charismatic in the U.S. and 150 million Catholic charismatic worldwide, only a part of the 600 million witnesses through Baptism in the Holy Spirit of all denominations worldwide! Many Catholics having experienced Baptism in the Spirit – this renewal of the sacraments of Baptism and Confirmation – have become more involved in their local parishes, community outreaches, teen ministry and missionary work. Pope John Paul II called the Renewal a "gift of the Holy Spirit to the Church" (March 14, 1992). And on the eve of Pentecost 2004 he stated, "Thanks to the Charismatic Movement, a multitude of Christians, men and women, young people and adults, have rediscovered Pentecost as a living reality in their daily lives. I hope that the spirituality of Pentecost will spread in the church as a renewed incentive to prayer, holiness, communion and proclamation." "The love of God has been poured into our hearts through the Holy Spirit who has been given to us." (Romans 5:5)

What an outpouring of the Spirit in 40 years!

2.

Doctrine

The Catholic Charismatic Renewal centers on the renewal of individual commitment to the person of Jesus Christ in his Church, through the power of the Holy Spirit, as in the day of Pentecost (Acts: 2). It begins by the re-anointing of the individual with the presence of the Holy Spirit, and it is primarily a renewal of the gifts received in the Sacraments of Baptism and Confirmation. It is a renewal in the elements of the Gospel that are central: The covenant love of the Father, the Lordship of Jesus, the power of the Spirit, sacramental and community life, prayer, Charisms and the necessity of evangelization.

The individuals in the Charismatic Renewal believe that they have been "filled" or "baptized" with the Holy Spirit, often through the laying on of hands. The signs of the "baptism" or "filling" may include wisdom, knowledge, faith, healing, mighty deeds (miracles), prophecy, discernment of spirits, speaking in tongues and interpretation of tongues. These are the nine spiritual gifts of the original Pentecost as Paul tells us in 1 Corinthians 12: 8-10.

Once having been baptized in the Spirit, the results are many. Along with the reception and use of the Charisms or gifts, people speak of a new and deeper personal knowledge and commitment to Jesus and his

Church. They find a new power and meaning in all kinds of prayer, a new love of the scripture, a new and deeper appreciation of the Church, of the sacraments, of the liturgy, of the Pope, of the Blessed Mother, of the Holy Sacrifice of the Mass, of the Rosary and of the Way of the Cross. The essence and life of any Charismatic is a life of joyfully praising the Lord and of service: helping his neighbor who is another Christ (Matthew 25:31-46).

The obvious result of all of this is that the Charismatic Catholic Renewal is "in" the Church and "for" the Church, not alongside the Church. It is at the heart of the Church, and has an important role in parish renewal. It is explosive, as anything moved by the fire and the hurricane wind of the Holy Spirit. Remember that in 23 years the Movement grew from a handful of Catholics in Pittsburgh into one that millions of Catholics now experience in over 200 nations. And this explosiveness of love and praise and service, can renew both your life and life of your parish too.

3.

What is a Prayer Group?

The meetings of the Charismatics are called "Prayer Groups", and they are usually full of joy and enthusiasm, praising the Lord and helping the brethren, singing and clapping hands, and even dancing. Their main purpose is to give glory to God our Father through our Lord Jesus Christ with the power of the Holy Spirit.

Most of the meetings consist of praising God with spontaneous prayers and singing, because "He, who prays singing, prays twice." These periods of prayer are punctuated by scripture readings, commentaries, sharing and prayers for the particular needs of individuals. There is also the specific practice of sharing any spiritual gift which any of the attendants might possess such as the gifts of wisdom, knowledge, faith, healing, mighty deeds (miracles), prophecy, and discernment of spirits, speaking in tongues, and interpretation of tongues... anything that may praise the Lord or be of help to the brethren. By the way, the gift of tongues is mentioned fifty-seven times in the New Testament. It is biblical, you know!

If you ever attend a Prayer Group and there is not joy and enthusiasm, it is a death Prayer Group! And, by the way, if in your life or your Catholic meetings there is not joy and enthusiasm, but boredom and tedium, the Charismatic Renewal may be a good remedy for not only your life but for your Catholic meetings as well, praise the Lord!

Actually, the meetings of Charismatics try to follow the recommendation of St. Paul: Not to get drunk with wine, but with the Holy Spirit, which is the best remedy for both your life and meetings:

- *"Do not get drunk with wine and the ruin that goes with it, but be filled with the Holy Spirit, as you sing psalms and hymns and spiritual songs among yourselves, praying and making melody to the Lord in your hearts, giving thanks always and for everything in the name of our Lord Jesus Christ to God the Father." (Ephesians 5:18-20)*
- *"When you assemble, one has a psalm, another an instruction, a revelation, or speaking in tongues, or interpreting what has been said in tongues. Everything should be done for building up the Church." (1 Corinthians 14: 26)*
- *"Rejoice always. Pray without ceasing. In all circumstances give thanks to God, for this is the will of God for you in Christ Jesus. Do not quench the Spirit. Do not despise prophetic utterances. Test everything; retain what is good. Refrain from every kind of evil." (1 Thessalonians 5: 16-22)*

The Prayer Meeting is usually an explosive one, and it is of the utmost importance that the Pastor or the priests of the Parish are interested and constantly aware of what is going on in the Prayer Group. Priests are always more than welcome to prayer meetings and if it is possible, one of the priests of the Parish should attend them regularly, or at least often. In fact, a priest of the Parish should be the main leader of each Prayer Group in the Parish.

The way of the Prayer Meeting should be lived in everyday life, at home, at work, and in the neighborhood. The Prayer Meeting is but an example of what should be our entire lives: the opportunity to recharge our batteries and to renew our lives again and again. Our lives should be an extension of the Prayer Meeting: praising the Lord always with joy and enthusiasm, giving thanks always and in all circumstances, praying constantly, serving others in their material and spiritual needs, and spreading the gospel with emphasis on evangelization.

II. Structure of a Prayer Group

The structure of a prayer group itself is a manifestation of the power of the Holy Spirit. It is not random, but made up of people who have been called to serve in different ways by the Spirit. Our prayer group is organized into different ministries, which allow individuals to serve for the benefit of the whole group. The word *ministry* originates from the Latin word ministrare, which means to *attend, serve, or manage*. Although each ministry is diverse, each one fulfills at least one of these roles. Individuals within each ministry share their own gifts, strengths and talents to help the group remain cohesive, organized, and most importantly God-centered.

1.

The Core Ministry

There are different ministries, but the same Lord.
(1 Corinthians 12:4-6)

The Core Ministry is the backbone and spiritual guide of our prayer group. The functions of the Core are diversified. Core Meetings take place every two weeks. At the beginning of each meeting, the Core Members immerse themselves in deep prayer, asking the Holy Spirit for guidance in making decisions and for the discernment to correctly handle any issues that may arise. This prayer time is taken very seriously as each member truly knows and believes that the Holy Spirit is an active participant, alive and in control of every decision that is to be made regarding the prayer group.

At the beginning of each New Year, it is the Core's responsibility to choose a special word or phrase from among the many suggestions given by the members. The selected phrase is chosen after much prayer and discussion. Examples from past years:

- *Trust in the Lord with all your heart; and lean not on your own understanding. (Proverbs 3:5-6)*

- *It was not you who chose me, but I who chose you to go and bear fruit that will last.*
- *Live completely in my presence.*
- *You are the light of the world. Your light must shine before all so that all may see goodness in your acts and give praise to our heavenly Father. (Acts 13:47)*
- *Be not afraid, for I am with you always. (Isaiah 43:1-3)*
- *See, I hold you in the palm of my hand, for you are mine.*
- *See, I make all things new. (Revelations 21:5)*
- *Seek me first; be still and know that I am God.*
- *Change my heart, O God.*
- *Fear is useless, what is needed is trust.*
- *Make us true servants.*
- *Acceptance with joy!*
- *I have chosen you.*
- *Barnabas, the Encourager.*

The phrase selected serves as a theme that resonates throughout the year. It is a foundation on which our prayer is built. I can still remember the first word we focused on. It was for us to be "Encouragers" as St. Barnabas was.

The Core Ministry also prepares the agendas for upcoming prayer meetings and chooses prayer group members who are willing and able to act as leaders. Each week one leader "shepherds" the meeting, acting as a spiritual guide for that evening. Leaders are scheduled by the Core on a rotating basis and each serves to lead the meeting once every four to six weeks. The leader sets the theme for the meeting, sometimes using just one word or phrase such as "Forgiveness," "Peace," "Be Still," or by sharing a personal spiritual experience. It is amazing how often the theme chosen is confirmed by others who have received the same inspiration through the Spirit, during the days preceding the meeting.

Another responsibility of the Core Ministry is to discern which members might be meant to serve in any one of our different ministries. This determination is based on each individual's gifts and talents and how it is thought they might best serve and contribute to the prayer group. It is not mandatory to be part of a ministry, and it is up to each individual to accept or decline the offer to join one.

Special events are also planned by the Core, such as our Annual Anniversary Mass and Celebration, Fat Tuesday Luncheon, and Baptism in the Holy Spirit, to name a few. To help fund these events, at the beginning of each New Year, the Core requests donations from members of the group. The funds collected are used to fund special events and joyous occasions as well acknowledge the sick and those who have died. The Core Ministry also sets aside a portion for charity and determines how contributions will be used during the year to help those in need.

Finally, the Core Ministry addresses any problems or disagreements which may arise within the group in a private and discreet manner. Such matters may include an individual's interpretation of a church law or passage of scripture. It is the responsibility of the Core to ensure that the prayer group always remains on track with church doctrine. The Core prays for the discernment to resolve such issues, and the wisdom to treat each person fairly and justly. Regardless of the problem or disagreement, the Core Ministry always gives love, understanding, friendship and forgiveness in abundance. Thanks to each and every member of our Core Ministry for your hard work and dedication, and for keeping us centered on the Lord.

2.

The Healing Ministry

At every moment pray in the Spirit,
using prayers and petitions of every sort.
Pray constantly and attentively for all in thy holy company.
(Ephesians 6:18)

The Healing Ministry ministers to those in physical or emotional distress. After each meeting, the members of the Healing Ministry make themselves available to pray over those in need of physical or emotional healing. They also visit those who are hospitalized or homebound and in need of healing prayer. A circle is formed around and hands are laid on the person to be prayed over. The members of this ministry then immerse themselves in intense prayer, praying for a prophetic word to sense the individual's problem and how it should be dealt with. The members of this ministry never refuse a request for healing prayer, regardless of the place or the hour. They are always ready to ease pain and give hope.

Another important service administered through the Healing Ministry is the Prayer Line. The Prayer Line is a group of members who accept telephone requests from individuals who need immediate intercessory prayer for themselves or for someone they know. The request for prayers for the individual is then relayed from person to person, by telephone, to each member of the Prayer Line. The members then stop what they are doing to petition and pray for the person in need. Through the prayers and faith of the Healing Ministry, many healings have taken place over the years.

Often when we ourselves are physically or emotionally sick, or weak, so is our faith. We may need others to carry our faith for us. In Luke 5:20, it was the paralyzed man's friends who lowered the mat through the crowds so he could be healed by Jesus. Seeing the faith of his friends, Jesus said, "My friend, your sins are forgiven you," and the man was healed. The Healing Ministry has faith for others when it becomes difficult for them to have it for themselves. They help keep faith and hope alive. "Blest are they who show mercy; mercy shall be theirs." (Matthew 5:7). Thank you members of the Healing Ministry, for you are true servants of our Lord.

3.

The Music Ministry

*God sent his singers upon the Earth with songs of gladness
that they might touch the hearts of humans
and bring them back to heaven again.
(Henry W. Longfellow)*

During our meetings, inspirational songs uplift our spirits, voices move us to praise, and music inspires us to give witness. Christened with the name, "His Notes," the Music Ministry is made up of people with diverse levels of music ability, but all with identical callings to praise him through music and song. Like our prayer, the music played and sung during our meetings is unplanned, but always inspired. Tapes, CD's and spontaneous songs abound. The beautiful simplicity of guitar, recorder, and tambourine, combined with voice, form a choir of heavenly angels singing glory to God in the highest. Our Music Ministry is present at all of our functions and they never disappoint us. They generously volunteer their talents at hospitals and nursing homes, giving pleasure and joy to the sick and elderly. We thank God for the gift of music and the joy it brings to each and every one of us! Thank you, Music Ministry, for sharing your gift of music with us.

4.

The Hospitality Ministry

Let all that you do be done in love.
(1 Corinthians 16:16)

When Jesus visited sisters Martha and Mary, it was Martha who performed the duties of housekeeping and hospitality, while Mary listened intently to Jesus, sitting near his feet. Jesus scolded Martha for not listening to his word, saying that Mary had "chosen the better portion." Our Hospitality Ministry has chosen both portions. During our meetings they join us in prayer and praise, listening intently to the word of God. But before and after our meetings, they work hard, preparing refreshments and cleaning up, so that we can share fellowship, friendship and food. The Hospitality Ministry also makes possible the many special events that take place during the year:

- *Annual Anniversary Mass and Celebration*
- *Fat Tuesday Luncheon (before Lent begins)*
- *Thanksgiving Eve Dinner*
- *Christmas Party*
- *Baptism in the Holy Spirit*

Like both Martha and Mary, the Hospitality Ministry helps us to enjoy the earthly nourishment of his bounty as well as the spiritual nourishment of his word. For this reason we must extend our heartfelt appreciation to the tireless members of this ministry. We never knew that earthly food could taste so heavenly. Thank you, Hospitality Ministry. Not only do you create feasts for our stomachs, but feasts for our eyes and souls as well.

5.

The Youth Ministry

Let the little children come to me.
Do not stop them, for it is such as these
to whom the kingdom of God belongs.
(Mark 10:14)

The Youth Ministry is a part of our Prayer Group that has changed throughout the years, depending on the number of young people involved at any given time. It has always been a blessing to have young people as part of our prayer community, and to watch them grow in the Spirit. The Youth Ministry gives young people the opportunity for fellowship with others their own age in a spiritual, grounded setting which emphasizes spirituality and morality. We welcome these young people for they are indeed the future. Many young people who started attending our prayer meeting in their teens are now adult members of our prayer group, and have children of their own. It is heartening and inspiring to see that faith and spirituality can be passed from one generation to the next. This is truly the greatest inheritance that a parent can give a child. As Jesus welcomed the little children, so do we welcome all young people to come and join us in prayer and fellowship. Thank you to the young members who have joined us in the past and are with us in the present. You remind us that there is hope for the future!

Through each of these ministries, the Holy Spirit has richly blessed us with many gifts. Musicians, writers, teachers, orators, healers and young people have become inspired to pursue their hidden talents because of the urging of the Holy Spirit and to use them to glorify God. We admire and appreciate each other's talents, and embrace each other's differences. We share joys, successes, sorrows and failures in equal portion. There are no ego trips here. We are all members of the Body of Christ, each with a purpose and each one necessary in some way for the well-being and success of the whole group. We praise God who has manifested himself to us in so many ways--even through the structure of our prayer group!

III. Format of a Prayer Meeting

Our God is a God of order, not disorder.
(1 Corinthians 14:33)

The Holy Spirit is a God of order, so at every prayer meeting there is an orderly approach to the way in which we pray. On any given night, our prayer meeting will most likely be attended by a different group of individuals because anyone is welcome to drop by and join us in prayer. Since the individuals in attendance may not be the same each week, a format is followed to prevent disorder and maintain consistency. This format is not rigid, because in no way do we wish to stifle the spontaneity and inspiration of the Holy Spirit. This allows us to enjoy both spontaneous and structured prayer within an organized format. For thirty years this format has proven to be successful and therefore it has changed little over time.

1.

Setup/Preparation -
Wednesdays about 7:30 PM

Prepare ye the way of the Lord.
(John the Baptist in Godspell)

Our weekly prayer meetings take place in a small room located in the lower level of our church. Each meeting begins with the simple arrangement of a group of folding chairs into a circle. A small table is moved to the center of the circle, and a candle, some rosary beads, a bible, and perhaps some other religious articles, are placed upon it. The candle at the center of the table is lit to represent the Light of Christ, the center of our lives. Members of the Music Ministry begin to unpack and set up their instruments and ready their sheet music. The Hospitality Ministry is already busy in the kitchen, setting up coffee, tea and refreshments to be enjoyed in fellowship after the meeting and one can already smell the coffee beginning to brew. Members old and new begin to trickle in and happily greet one another. Any newcomers are immediately acknowledged and greeted with a warm welcome to put them at ease in their new surroundings. After our greetings to both new and old are complete, the Hospitality Ministry has completed their preparations, and the Music Ministry is ready, everyone takes a place in the circle of chairs. A once cold and empty church room, through the simple gathering together of a table, a few folding chairs, and a humble group of people, has been transformed to us, into a chapel, a temple, a cathedral of prayer.

2.

The Rosary -
Wednesdays at 8:00 PM

Pray for us sinners.
(The Hail Mary)

Since our prayer group is dedicated to the Intercession of Mary, Cause of Our Joy, it is most fitting that we begin every meeting with the recitation of the Rosary. The Rosary is not only a devotion for all seasons but an ideal meditation on the life and works of our Lord, Jesus Christ. We pray for the intercession of Mary on our behalf to bring us closer to her son, Jesus. Each week a specific member leads the group in the recitation of five decades of the Rosary. If that member is not present, another member will lead us in the Rosary for that week. During the recitation of the Rosary more faithful friends slowly drift in, filling the empty seats to complete our prayer circle, joining us in prayer and preparation for the meeting.

3.
Leader's Deliverance Prayer - Wednesdays about 8:15 PM

Deliver us from evil. Amen
(The Lord's Prayer)

Following the recitation of the Rosary, the leader for that evening's meeting stands and selects one person from the group to pray over him or her. All present are asked to extend a hand prayerfully toward the leader and then silently join in lifting up that person in a deliverance prayer. Although each week's leader is different, the purpose of the deliverance prayer is always the same: to ask the Lord to bestow the leader with the grace and wisdom necessary to shepherd us through the meeting, and most importantly, to request that anything not from God be removed from our midst. Such things might include stress, anxiety, hatred, and jealousy. We then invoke the Spirit of the living God to fall afresh on us. We ask the Spirit of the living God to mold us. Fill us. Use us. Heal us and teach us.

After the deliverance prayer, the leader welcomes everyone. If newcomers are present, the leader acknowledges them, welcomes them and then gives a brief synopsis of what will take place during the meeting to familiarize them with the format of our meeting. We are now ready to begin.

4.

Opening Prayer -
Wednesdays about 8:25 PM

As incense rises up to the heavens, so shall your prayers.
(Revelations 8:4)

The leader begins with an opening prayer. The leader's opening prayer is meant to help us unwind, settle down and focus, so that we can put aside any distractions that might be invading our peace of mind and might prevent us from focusing on the Lord. In order to completely immerse ourselves in prayer, and to reap its fullest benefit, we need to free our minds of the encumbrances of daily life that prevent us from concentrating on our Lord. This is not always easy, but is very important if we are to fully experience the Lord's presence at our meeting. It is a vital role of the leader to help us accomplish this. The leader's opening prayer each week reminds us for what purpose we have gathered and how we must prioritize our thoughts and concerns to make our prayer time and meeting, both individually and as a group, as productive as possible.

Because the meeting's leader varies each week, so does the opening prayer, but its theme is always consistent: we are thankful that we have all been brought together in prayer; we ask God to make our ears and hearts open to his word; we ask that we may have a fruitful meeting; we ask for his blessing upon each of us and our families; we thank God for all of his blessings in our lives; we give thanks for each other; and we give thanks for this fellowship, because it is through his word that we are strengthened.

5.
Leader's Witness -
Wednesdays about 8:30 PM

Before all men you are to be his witness to what you have seen and heard.
(Acts 22:15)

After the opening prayer, the leader gives witness to how the Lord has touched him or her in a special way since our last meeting. It might be the revelation of how God worked through a recent event in his or her life, or a line of scripture through which God revealed his word to the leader, that will set the theme for the rest of the meeting. This is when the word of God becomes truly alive and living to us. After hearing the leader's witness, others present confirm the spiritual message, based on their own experiences and personal revelations over the past week. Week after week, meeting after meeting, the Holy Spirit will impress upon our hearts that the words spoken by the leader are important words for us to hear, because other members then validate what the leader has said when they share witness of God's intercession in their own lives, later in the meeting.

6.

Opening Hymn -
Wednesdays about 8:35 PM

Sing praise to the Lord.
(Isaiah 12:5)

It is now time to lift our voices in song, praise, thanksgiving. The opening hymn is a song of praise that inspires us to worship God from whom all blessings flow. Often the leader selects the hymn. Other times, the Music Ministry will select a hymn which ties in with the theme of the leader's witness statement. Our musical selections come from a wide array of sources, and many of the songs we sing have been inspired by the Spirit and composed by the talented members of our own Music Ministry. Regardless of their source, all of our musical selections have one purpose: to glorify and praise God through music, voice and song.

7.

Praise and Thanksgiving -
Wednesdays about 8:40 PM

Enter his gates with thanksgiving and his courts with praise.
(Psalm 100)

After the opening hymn, we again use our voices to pay homage and make a joyful noise unto the Lord for all that he has given us, because all that we are or ever hope to be, we owe to him. This is the opportunity to express to God anything that may be in our minds and hearts that evening. We stand in our circle with arms uplifted unto the Lord to praise and thank him for all with which he has blessed us. We are standing on holy ground and he is in our midst. This is the time for us to express, either silently or out loud, but simultaneously, each in our own way, our thanks to him who is the center of our life. Some will speak in tongues; others will have a word of discernment; some will prophesy; and some may be healed. This usually lasts about 20 minutes and sets the tone for us to further enter into the Lord's presence.

8.

Inspired Thoughts and Prayerful Reflections -
Wednesdays about 9:00 PM

All scripture is inspired of God and is useful for teaching.
(2 Timothy 3:16)

This is truly the heart of our prayer meeting. It is the time when we read scripture, sing hymns, speak prophecies and share words of knowledge and confirmation of healings with one another. With the theme of the leader's witness freshly in mind, members now share their own witness to tell of how God has revealed himself to them and done marvelous things in their own lives over the past week. During this hour, the most miraculous part of the meeting, it becomes apparent to us that God has revealed to us his same word separately in our everyday lives, and again here, together as a group. It is truly a manifestation of the fruits of our individual and united prayer and a testament to its power. This confirmation of God's word, begun with our leader's witness and validated by the other members of our group during this part of the meeting, strengthens us both as individuals and as a group. It reinforces that the word of God is truly the living word and that God is an active participant in our everyday lives if we allow him to be and are open to him.

9.

Meditation Hymn -
Wednesdays about 9:55 PM

Let the words of my mouth and the meditation of my heart
be acceptable in thy sight, O God.
(Psalms 19:14)

To help us meditate on the witnesses given and the confirmations shared during the heart of our meeting, the Music Ministry sings an inspirational hymn which allows members to reflect on what we have just shared with one another. This gives us the opportunity to think about the common messages that ran through the witnesses given by the leader, and all those present. We are opening our minds to discern the word he is trying to impress upon our hearts tonight. We meditate upon how this word pertains to us, not only in each of our personal lives, but in our collective lives as part of this prayer group.

10.

Petition Time -
Wednesdays about 10:00 PM

Ask and you shall receive.
(1 John 3:22)

As our meeting begins to draw to a close, our final thoughts are put toward those who are in need and also for those who ask for our prayers. It is during this time that we lift our petitions up to God, humbly and fervently asking Our Lord to hear them.

There are two types of petitions. General petitions are addressed first. General petitions offer the opportunity for us to pray for those in need, both those that are known and unknown to us. We begin with our own families and community, and then extend our prayers to petition for the needs of the wider world, based on recent events. Anyone may put forth a petition during this time, after which all members join together in prayer for the petition requested.

Personal petitions are a very important part of our meeting. Each person requests prayers from the rest of the group for a family member, friend, themselves, or for a very specific need. After each petition is announced, all present sit silently for a few moments, praying deeply either silently or out loud for the specific need. During this time, a certain sense of aura and sacredness fills the meeting as we humbly direct our prayers to God our Father, Jesus His Son, the Holy Spirit and for the intercession of the Blessed Mother. We pray as a group for our own personal needs, but also for the needs of one another.

11.

Closing Prayer -
Wednesdays about 10:05 PM

All good things must come to an end.
(English Proverb)

Oftentimes when we are concluding the meeting, we pray together One Our Father, One Hail Mary and the Glory Be as our final prayer. Other times, when appropriate, a closing prayer is chosen in keeping with the theme of the meeting. Either way, the purpose of this final prayer is to thank him this meeting and for having brought us together once again in united prayer; to pray that the Spirit will fortify each of us in our faith during the coming week; to ask for the strength to proceed in the world as role models of Christian faith, that our example may be an inspiration to draw others closer to God; and to ask that God watch over each of us, all of us and our families over the coming week.

12.

Announcements -
Wednesdays about 10:10 PM

Give ear, listen humbly, for the Lord speaks.
(Jeremiah 13:15)

General announcements such as upcoming events are discussed during this part of the meeting. This might include upcoming Core Meetings, retreats, and events both within the prayer group and the parish. Anyone who has information or resources that might be of interest to other members of the group is welcome to share it at this time.

13.

Closing Hymn -
Wednesdays about 10:15 PM

My heart exults and with my song I give him thanks.
(Psalms 28:7)

Our final prayer for the evening is one in which we lift our voices together in unison before we depart from one another. We go forth by praising him in song. The hymn is usually selected spontaneously by the Music Ministry based on the theme of the witnesses shared throughout the course of the meeting. For the final time of the evening, the Music Ministry once again leads us in song as we join our voices together in praise.

14.

Healing Ministry Intercessory Prayer - Wednesdays about 10:20 PM

Thus says the Lord the God of your forefather David:
I have heard your prayer and seen your tears. I will heal you.
(2 Kings 20:5)

At this time, for those who request it, the Healing Ministry will provide intercessory prayer for physical or emotional healing. This does occur from time to time during one of our meetings. If someone in attendance requests it, whichever members present that are part of the Healing Ministry will avail themselves to that person. The prayers offered are for the individual's specific need or problem, and these prayers are offered in private and on a confidential basis. The members of the Healing Ministry will go off to a separate room and pray for approximately 15 minutes over the person in need, laying hands upon them, and praying intensely. The members also often receive a prophetic word to help them sense the individual's problem and how it should be dealt with.

15.

Fellowship - Wednesdays about 10:20 PM

Lord, how good that we are here.
(Matthew 17:4)

Fellowship is the time when our members come together to relax, catch up with one another, get to know new arrivals, share coffee and cake, and discuss how they were touched by the Holy Spirit during the meeting. We take this time before we part for the week, to share with each other the events in our personal lives that occurred during the previous week. We give each other comfort and encouragement as we share the joys and sorrows of life. We value and cherish one another. We are grateful for the support we give each other through our common faith and fellowship in Christ.

16.

Good Night and God Bless - Wednesdays about 10:45 PM

Finally, brothers, good-bye.
Aim for perfection, listen to my appeal, be of one mind, live in peace.
And the God of love and peace will be with you.
(2 Corinthians 13:11)

As we begin to disperse, the instruments are put back into their cases, the sheet music is once again gathered up, and our Hospitality Ministry begins clean up. We begin to say our goodbyes for the week. "Go with God!" is our wish for one another. See you next week, be the good Lord willing!

17.

Clean Up and Close Up -
Wednesdays about 10:50 PM

Cleanliness is next to Godliness.
(John Wesley)

For all of our thirty years, we have been fortunate to have the use of our church hall, and in gratefulness for the use of it, strive to leave it as we found it. Floors are swept. Coffee pots are emptied and cleaned, and tabletops are cleared. Rosaries are put away, candles blown out, Bibles tucked away, and tables wiped down. Finally, the circle of chairs is dismantled, then folded and restacked in the proper place, until next Wednesday at Eight.

IV. Experience Your Own

Prayer Meeting

Now that you are familiar with the format of a prayer meeting, you are ready to experience your own. This can take place either individually or as a group. If you are praying alone, try scheduling your prayer time for 8:00 PM on Wednesdays, so that you will be spiritually joining us in fellowship. If this is not possible, any time of day that gives you uninterrupted prayer time is suitable.

On the following pages are step-by-step instructions to guide you through. Whether you are praying alone or with others, adjust the format accordingly, using this section as a framework to guide you. Use this guide in the same way you would use a prayer missal to follow the Sunday Mass.

The heart of any one of our meetings is the portion we refer to as "Inspired Thoughts and Prayerful Reflections." Fifty two sets of partnered prayers to use during this portion of prayer have been provided in Section V, the next section of this book. For convenience, the first set has been included in the missal. Each time that you pray with us, you may read one set of these prayers. If you prefer, you can also open the Bible and read a passage, and then reflect on its meaning and relevance to your life. Indeed, the hymns, prayers and reflections are only suggestions to guide you as you get started. Feel free to use your own. *You can easily identify all suggested hymns, prayers and meditations; they are identified in italic.*

Remember that the missal on the following pages is provided as a framework to help you structure your own prayer in the context of a prayer meeting. Allow the Spirit to work through you. Open your heart. Open your mind. Listen to his voice. Make the prayer time truly your own, as no doubt the Holy Spirit will move you to do.

Prayer Missal

1. <u>Setup/Preparation</u>

Set up a special place in your home where you will not be disturbed. Choose a comfortable chair, near a well-lit, but subtle lamp. Have a small table nearby on which you can place a few of your favorite religious articles, and a set of Rosary beads. A candle can be placed in the center of the table and lit, to represent the Light of Christ. For inspiration, you might also have a tape or CD player cued up to three of your favorite hymns for the Opening, Meditation and Closing Hymns. Keep a spiritual journey handy so that you can jot down any revelations that might occur to you during prayer time.

Put all of the day's problems and activities out of your mind. Set aside any distractions that might be invading your peace of mind. Concentrate only on the presence of the Holy Spirit dwelling within you. This is very important in order to fully experience the Lord's presence.

2. <u>Recite the Rosary.</u>

3. <u>Leader's Deliverance Prayer</u>

Pray for the Lord's protection against any evil that might be present.

Dear God:

We prayerfully ask that if there is anything or anyone in this holy place that is not of you, please remove it and bind it to yourself. Empty from us any anxiety, nervousness or unpleasant thoughts that might distract us from focusing on being fully in your presence. We place our families, friends, community, members of our parish, and possessions under your holy protection. Fill us with your love, peace, joy and holiness. Bless this meeting and make it fruitful so that we may go forth, filled with your love, peace, and joy, to spread the Good News to all we meet. Amen.

4. <u>Opening Prayer</u>

Dear Father:

All praise and thanksgiving is yours, most precious God. All that we have and possess is yours, almighty Father. You are the Creator of all that we are or ever hope to be. If we write a song or a book, you are the inspiration. If we speak eloquently and profoundly, you are the breath of our voice. If we lay hands on someone and the person is healed, it is only because the power has come from you, almighty God. If we are filled with discernment, wisdom or prophecy, it is only because your Holy Spirit has given us instruction. Lord, it is not due to our credit that we do all these things, but to your enormous generosity in using us as your servants. We pray that we will always be loyal to your call. We pray that we will always be filled with humility, knowing that without you, we are nothing.

There is only one request that we ask of you—that we may always remain in your good grace and continue to serve you according to your holy will. Master, teach us your ways! You alone have the words of everlasting life. Open our ears, open our eyes, and open our hearts to your holy truth. Your ways are not the ways of the world. Take our egos from us and melt them and mold them into your mind and thoughts. Give us courage to speak what mysteries you reveal to us. Correct our faults and take from us anything that is not of your holiness. If we can inspire those around us to draw closer to you, if we can ease someone's pain, if we can give encouragement, if we can bring hope, if we can be an example of your love, if we can be true Christians in every sense of the word, then we will not have lived in vain. Gracious God, protect us from the evil one. Watch over us, Lord; guard our souls. Our one desire is to be with you through all eternity.

We thank you for the joy that fills us when we have done something that is pleasing in your sight. It is a joy that cannot come from the world. It is a divine joy! It is a joy that comes from knowing that it is more blessed to give than to receive. We pray for those who have never experienced being joyful givers. It is a heaven-sent gift from you! It is one more reason to give you thanks and praise.

Lord, fill our existence with yourself. You must increase and we must decrease. Merciful God, have pity on us. Hear our pleas and listen to our prayer. We are unworthy to have been chosen, but because you have chosen us, we are worthy in your sight. Lord, whatever way you choose to use us to bear fruit, we are your humble servants. Take from us our pride in whatever we may accomplish. Let the praise and the glory be yours forever and ever, for you are the true vine and we are only the branches. Apart from you, we can do nothing. Amen.

5. <u>Leader's Witness</u>

The leader shares with the rest of the group the way the Lord has worked in his or her life recently by discussing a recent event, encounter, triumph or struggle and how God's presence was felt during it. If praying alone, reflect on how he has shown himself to be present in your own life, whether through struggles or triumphs, large or small. Think of the ways he may have spoken to you, whether it was through an encounter with someone you met this week, a line of scripture or literature that you may have read, or any other incident through which God has made a connection to your life and shown himself to be present to you. The more you become open to it, the more easily you will recognize how God works through the people and things that we encounter in our everyday lives to speak to us and to reveal to us that he is truly an active participant in our lives.

6. <u>Opening Hymn</u>

Sing or play an appropriate hymn, ideally one that ties in with the witness shared.

Praise to the Lord *(Lobe Den Herren)*

Praise to the Lord, the Almighty, the King of creation.
O my soul praise him, for he is our health and salvation.
All you who hear, now to his altar draw near;
Join in profound adoration.

Praise to the Lord, let us offer our gifts at the altar.
Let not our sins and offenses now cause us to falter.
Christ the High Priest, bids us all join in his feast.
Victim's with him on the altar.

Praise to the Lord, O let all that is in us adore him.
All that has life and breath come now, in praises before him.
Let the "Amen," sound from his people again.
Now as we worship before him.

7. <u>Praise and Thanksgiving</u>

Kneel, sit or stand, and raise your arms in praise and thanksgiving to the Lord either silently or verbally, in your own words. In every circumstance, even our own trials, if we search hard enough, we can find something for which to be grateful and give thanks for. Search your heart for those things and praise him.

8. <u>Inspired Thoughts and Prayerful Reflections</u>

It is time to give witness to how, with God's help, we overcome adversity, cope with illness, survive hardships and celebrate joys in our lives. Become conscious of how the Holy Spirit has been an active participant during every experience in your life. To help you do this, following is the first of the Fifty-two Inspired Thoughts and Prayerful Reflections in the next section of this book. As you read the partnered prayers, consider the relevance of these words to your own life. You may also open the bible and select a passage that has meaning and significance to you.

Week One
Inspired Thought

A Special Night! A New Year! A New Beginning
(Inspired by the Millennium 2000)

"The cross we carry is never as heavy as the chains from which we were freed."
-Anonymous

I saw a banquet table covered with food and many people sitting around it. The scene reminded me of the Passover Feast, but at the head of the table, instead of Moses, stood Jesus. It was not Passover, but New Year's Eve. It was a celebration of us all entering into the Millennium. A hand was raised at the table, and a voice spoke to Jesus. "Why is this night different from any other night?" Jesus answered, "Slaves will be freed; chains will be broken. Leave the shackles that bind you to the old century behind. You are about to enter the door into the year of 2000, the new Millennium, as a new creation, unbound. The Covenant that I wish to make is that you be free from the chains of the world that would separate you from me. You will have the strength to free yourselves from these chains, because I am with you at all times and with me all things are possible.

Week One
Prayerful Reflection

My Children:

Out with the old year and the old you; in with the New Year and the new you. You are to be a new creation. You must lay aside your former way of life and acquire a new and spiritual way of thinking:

Out with all that leads to sinfulness; in with all that leads to holiness.
Out with past grievances; in with forgiveness.
Out with confusion; in with simplicity.
Out with anxiety; in with peace.
Out with materialism; in with spirituality.
Out with past hurts; in with healing.
Out with division; in with wholeness.
Out with anger; in with love.

In order to accomplish this, you must trust me completely. I ask you to surrender your family and friends to me. Do not give up on them, simply surrender them to me. I will take care of them. They too are my children. I love them and wish them to be saved. Surrender your ambitions, jobs and future to me. Leave them in my hands and I will bless you with the discernment that you need to make the right choices. Surrender your reputation to me. What people say and think is not important to me. You are precious in my sight and that is all that should concern you. Surrender your possessions to me so that you can truly say you have given all to me and everything you have is mine. I will return them to you in abundance. Surrender your social life, recreation and amusements to me, and I will fill you with a joy that you could never imagine exists. Surrender your relationships to me and I will give you insight as to what you need to make them harmonious.

You know neither the time nor the hour in which you will be called to appear before me. Now is the acceptable time for you to change. Out with all old habits that lead to sin and destruction; in with all new virtues that lead to peace and holiness. Remember, I instruct you because I love you and want what is best for you. You are to be a new creation. Out with the old you and in with the new you!

After reading your partnered prayers or selected passage, take a few moments to reflect on how the Lord is speaking to you. Think back over the past week and how the passage you read applies to you personally. Think about the recent happenings in your life. Meditate on how they might connect with the message that is being conveyed. Take some time to interpret the relevance of the passage to you personally. Ask the Spirit to keep your mind and heart open to any word of consolation, encouragement or confirmation that he might have for you.

9. <u>Meditation Hymn</u>

Play or sing a song of your choice. Reflect on the ways that the Lord is trying to speak to you. Open up your heart and mind to discern the message he has for you.

Amazing Grace

Amazing grace, how sweet the sound,
That saved and set me free.
I once was lost, but now am found,
Was blind, but now I see.

'Twas grace that taught my heart to fear,
And grace my fear relieved.
How precious did that grace appear,
The hour I first believed.

10. Petition Time

Ask and ye shall receive. Ask God for the needs of others and for your own needs, and for the grace to accept his will for you.

General Petitions

During this time, petition for the needs of your own families and community, and then extend to the needs of the wider world, based on the past week's events.

- *We pray for all of our members and also for those who could not be here with us tonight. (Lord, hear our prayer.)*
- *We pray for our families and friends. (Lord, hear our prayer.)*
- *We pray for the Pope, Cardinals, Bishops, Brothers, Sisters, Deacons, and religious communities and denominations, and all lay people who are called upon to spread the Gospel. (Lord, hear our prayer.)*
- *We pray for those who are physically, mentally and spiritually ill. (Lord, hear our prayer.)*

- *We pray for all the children of the world. (Lord, hear our prayer.)*
- *We pray that you fill us with your Holy Spirit so that we may go forth in courage and holiness to profess your word to those who do not know you. (Lord, hear our prayer.)*

Personal Petitions

Pray out loud or silently for personal petitions you would like to ask of the Lord. Pray as a group for the needs of one another, both those petitions that are expressed out loud as well as those petitions that are requested silently.

Lord, thank you for hearing the petitions we ask for ourselves and also those we ask for others. Please hear the prayers we have spoken out loud as well as those we have hidden in the recesses of our hearts. We know that you hear all our prayers, and we believe you will answer them in your own time, according to your holy will. All glory be to the Father, and to the Son and to the Holy Spirit. Amen.

11. <u>Closing Prayer</u>

Dear Father:

Before we say goodnight to you and to each other, we wish to give you thanks and praise for blessing us with this wonderful gift of knowing you in a personal and intimate fashion. There are so many who do not know you, and at times feel that their lives have no purpose. They feel that life is meaningless to them. We lift these people up to you in prayer.

Teach us to be more like Mary, not only serving in the kitchen, but giving us the grace to listen to your words attentively at your feet, so that we can share them with those who hunger to know you. Help us to keep you near when we are bombarded with the unimportant details that arise each day as we face our daily tasks.

Teach and help us to understand the true meaning of your miraculous gift to us, your word becoming flesh. For reasons we cannot even begin to fathom, you sent your Son to speak and walk among us. How much love and forgiveness you have shown us, sacrificing him so that we might regain heaven.

Give us hearts of flesh in order that we may love others as you have loved us. Help us to love and forgive all who cross our path, so that we may learn to deal with the trials that come with being part of a family. When you call us to minister to those who are sick, when we are faced with financial problems, when we are asked to pardon those who have hurt or betrayed us, help us to remember that we, ourselves, are not perfect. You alone are our peace and comfort amidst the turmoil that comes with daily living. Protect and guide us in our comings and goings.

Give us the discernment to not place importance on things of this world, which will all pass away. Instead, instill in our hearts and minds the knowledge that your words are everlasting and shall never pass away.

Instill in us a love toward others that surpasses all understanding. Help us to realize that it is only through love of you and others that we will conquer the evil in the world.

O Lord, let us never take you for granted. Let us always be aware of your presence in our lives, for without you, we can do nothing. Help us to celebrate your love during this coming week, as we pray for our families, friends and each one of us here tonight. We thank you and ask you to protect and guide us as we go forth to honor and serve you all the days of our lives. Amen.

12. **Announcements**

Announce any upcoming events or resources that might be useful to other members. Any member who has information that might be beneficial to others in the group is encouraged to share it at this time.

13. **Closing Hymn**

The closing hymn marks the formal end of the meeting. Select and play or sing a hymn of your choice.

Joyful, Joyful, We Adore Thee

Joyful, joyful, we adore thee,
God of glory, Lord of Love;
Hearts unfold like flow'rs before thee,
Praising thee, their sun above.

Melt the clouds of sins and sadness;
Drive the dark of doubt away;
Giver of immortal gladness,
Fill us with the light of day.

14. **Healing Ministry Intercessory Prayer**

If you are part of a group that has an established Healing Ministry, and there have been requests for intercessory prayer, it is during this time that this prayer is administered. If you are praying alone and are in need of spiritual or physical healing, gently cross your arms and embrace yourself; immerse yourself in prayer; pray that the hands of Jesus may touch you and heal you and that his arms enfold you and comfort you.

15.   <u>Fellowship</u>

Fellowship with others who share our faith strengthens us in our own faith. Sharing coffee, cake and casual conversation outside of regular prayer time strengthens the bonds of faith and friendship between those that pray together.

16.   <u>**Good Night and God Bless**</u>

It is time to say goodnight, and bid one another farewell, until we meet again.

17.   <u>**Clean Up and Close Up**</u>

It is time to put away the rosaries, close the Bible, and carefully tuck all items away in their rightful places in anticipation of your next prayer meeting.

Meditation:
Your First Prayer Meeting

A prayer meeting can evoke many emotions. This meditation can help you recognize the many feelings that attending a first Prayer Meeting can awaken.

Perhaps you came to our prayer meeting expecting great things and were disappointed when your expectations went unfulfilled. Then slowly you discovered a new vision, that of a personal relationship with the Lord, a relationship that you never imagined could exist. He became real to you!

Perhaps you came to our prayer meeting out of curiosity, but your curiosity was not satisfied. Then suddenly, you discovered gifts inside of you, gifts released through the power of his Holy Spirit. You became filled with power from on high!

Perhaps you came to our prayer meeting anticipating that something special would happen, but all you felt was frustration; maybe someone got on your nerves that night. But then you settled in, became attentive to the readings and suddenly, your eyes and ears were opened to the unexpected. Holy Scripture came alive, revealing to you the mysteries of his kingdom!

Perhaps you came to our prayer meeting seeking the exceptional, the extraordinary, maybe a miracle; but all was plain and simple. And then he revealed to you that his greatest miracles are achieved by using the common and the ordinary!

Perhaps you came to our prayer meeting with many questions and found no answers, but you listened when he said, "Seek and you will find." With a sudden clarity which can only come from him, what was hidden became revealed to you!

Perhaps you came to our prayer meeting looking for a change of scenery, a new idea, an inspiration; but not finding any, you walked away in frustration, until you noticed the greatest change of all—the change in your heart.

Perhaps you came to our prayer meeting thinking that he would use you to contribute something great or heroic; that maybe you would move someone with a stupendous act or deed. And then he whispered to you, "Do only the simple, but do it in a big way!"

Perhaps you came to our prayer meeting with a burning desire to pray and found only emptiness. Then he inspired you with a call to be still and listen, for he is God and knows all that you need.

Perhaps you came to our prayer meeting for a rest, a chance to get away for a while, but the night you came, there was not even a chair for you to sit on. Then you discovered that you were standing on hallowed ground, because where two or more are gathered, he is in their midst!

Perhaps you came to our prayer meeting for one reason or for many, but found nothing for which you came, and then, all of a sudden, you were filled with an unexplainable joy. All those things you thought you needed you really didn't need. He gave you the one thing you truly did need; he gave you himself, the greatest of all miracles and in finding him, you found yourself!

Part V. Fifty-Two Inspired Thoughts and

Prayerful Reflections

Week One
Inspired Thought

A Special Night! A New Year! A New Beginning!
(Inspired by the New Millennium 2000)

The cross we carry is never as heavy
as the chains from which we were freed!
(Anonymous)

I saw a banquet table covered with food and many people sitting around it. The scene reminded me of the Passover Feast but at the head of the table instead of Moses, stood Jesus. It was not Passover but New Year's Eve. It was a celebration of us all entering into the Millennium. A hand was raised at the table and a voice spoke to Jesus. "Why is this night different from any other night?" Jesus answered, "Slaves will be freed; chains will be broken. Leave the shackles that bind you to the old century behind. You are about to enter the door into the year of 2000, the new Millennium, as a new creation, unbound. The covenant that I wish to make is that you be free from the chains of the world that would separate you from me. You will have the strength to free yourselves from these chains, because I am with you at all times, and with me, all things are possible."

Week One
Prayerful Reflection

My Children,

Out with the old year and the old you; in with the New Year and the new you. You are to be a new creation. You must lay aside your former way of life and acquire a new and spiritual way of thinking.

> Out with all that leads to sinfulness; in with all that leads to holiness.
> Out with all past grievances; in with forgiveness.
> Out with confusion; in with simplicity.
> Out with anxiety; in with peace.
> Out with materialism; in with spirituality.
> Out with past hurts; in with healing.
> Out with division; in with wholeness.
> Out with anger; in with love.

In order to accomplish this you must trust me completely. I ask you to surrender your family and friends to me. Do not give up on them; simply surrender them to me. I will take care of them. They too, are my children. I love them and wish them to be saved. Surrender your ambitions, jobs and future to me. Leave these in my hands and I will bless you with the discernment you need to make the right choices. Surrender your reputation to me. What people say and think about you is not important to me. You are precious in my sight and that is all that should concern you. Surrender your possessions to me so that you can truly say you have given all to me and everything you have is mine. I will return them to you in abundance. Surrender your social life, recreation, and amusements to me and I will fill you with a joy that you can never imagine. Surrender your relationships to me and I will give you insight as to what you need to make them harmonious.

You know neither the time nor the hour in which you will be called to appear before me. Now is the acceptable time for you to change. Out with all old habits that lead to sin and destruction; in with all new virtues that lead to peace and holiness. Remember, I instruct you because I love you and want what is best for you. You are to be a new creation. Out with the old you and in with the new you!

Week Two
Inspired Thought

Disciples of Today

Make me understand the way of your precepts,
and I will meditate on your wondrous works!
(Psalms 119:27)

Jesus is calling us to be the disciples of today. But is Jesus reprimanding us, "How long must I be with you before you understand?" When will we finally get it? Some of us have been members of a prayer group for many years. We have heard and read his words and his promises. Do we truly believe we have the power and authority he says we do? Have we claimed and practiced the faith that he has willed to us?

Tonight I heard Jesus say to us, "Grow up – when you were children, you acted and thought as children, but now you must put away childish things. You must be responsible and believing adults. You must be steadfast and have courage. Act as if you have faith and faith will be given to you in abundance."

We read in the gospel of Luke about a woman who keeps pleading for justice to be served. She keeps annoying an evil judge until she finally wears him down to help her. There is a moral here. Jesus is telling us that if even an evil judge can be worn down like that, won't God give justice to his people when they plead with him day and night? Yes, he will answer his people, but the question is: When the Son of Man comes, will he find anyone with faith on the earth? Do we have the persistence of faith necessary to become his disciples of today?

Let our prayer ring out to him: "Lord, we do believe, but help us overcome our unbelief. Lord, we do have faith, but help our faith to increase. Lord, help us to become true disciples of today according to your holy will. Amen!"

Week Two
Prayerful Reflection

My Children,

Such light, such joy flows out from this place. It affects all those who come here. You do not have to try hard to help them. Just love them, welcome them, shower a little kindness on them, and you will make a difference in their lives.

Love is God. When you give them love, you give them God and that allows my Father to do his work. I may have put the impulse into someone's despairing heart to visit your prayer group tonight. If you have not welcomed them, think how you have failed my Father.

I wish to use you. I need you. My broken world needs you. Many a weary and troubled heart will be gladdened by you and draw nearer to me because of you.

The Christian life – life with me – is a love story. All you need you will find in me: the soul's lover; the soul's friend; father; mother; comrade. Try me. You cannot make too many demands upon me. Claim what is yours – healing, power, joy, love; whatever you need, I will supply. Faith is the key that unlocks the storehouse which is filled with gifts for each of you.

I am filled with such joy when one of my lost sheep enters the portals of your prayer group and is welcomed. Continue your good works, and your prayer community will thrive because of my abundant blessings on you all.

Week Three
Inspired Thought

The Fifth Gospel

The Spirit of the Lord is upon me,
because he has anointed me to bring Good News!
(Luke 4:18)

We cannot just read and preach the gospel. We must believe and live the gospel. There are four gospels: Matthew, Mark, Luke and John, but in reality, there are five gospels. We are the fifth gospel. We have been called to live our lives so that this gospel becomes visible. Just as the purpose of the windmill is to make visible the presence of the wind, our purpose in becoming the fifth gospel is to make visible the presence of God to others.

It seems hard to believe that in this day and age, there are still people whom we come in contact with, even those living close to us, who have never opened a Bible. We assume everyone has heard the word proclaimed from the altar, yet there are many who do not attend a place of worship. We often take for granted that everyone knows and understands what God did for us through Jesus Christ. In this day of vast communication, how can anyone not have heard the Good News? Yet proclaiming the word is an ongoing work. "Let your light shine before all so they may see your good works and give glory to your Father in heaven." And if we speak because we truly believe what we have learned from the Lord, our words will be spoken with passion and they will stir the imagination and satisfy the hunger of those who are searching for something they know is missing from their lives.

The gospels are the voice of God made visible. We cannot add or detract from these sacred writings. Their words have been carried down from generation to generation for two thousand years. Now it is our turn to pass the flame to the next generation. It is no less a challenge today than it was in the past. Today, we have many obstacles to overcome. There is a great distance between our speaking the word and having others be open to hearing the word. Have you ever tried to talk to someone about something of importance when they were watching a favorite television show or reading a book or being involved in some other pursuit? It is really impossible to get through to them. Their minds and thoughts are elsewhere.

Although we are living in an era of great technological progress, communication between human beings seems to be sadly neglected. We are either being bombarded with words or we are bombarding others with words. There is no dialogue. No back and forth. No communication. Even with God, we do all the talking. We are too anxious, too much in a hurry!

Yet, we are the fifth gospel. Listen to what scripture tells us in Romans, Chapter 10: "Everyone who calls out to the Lord for help will be saved." But how can people call out to him for help if they do not believe? And how can they believe if they have not heard the message? And how can they hear the message if it is not proclaimed? And how can the message be proclaimed if the messengers are not sent out? Scripture reminds us, "How beautiful are the feet of those who announce the Good News!"

We are the fifth gospel. This was commanded by our Lord himself in Mark, Chapter 28. Jesus said to the eleven disciples: "Full authority has been given to me both in heaven and on Earth; go, therefore, and make disciples of all the nations. Baptize them in the name of the Father, and of the Son, and of the Holy Spirit. Teach them to carry out everything I have commanded you. And know that I am with you always until the end of the world."

We must pray to have a close relationship with God so that we can be taught by him. We must study the Bible and try to meditate on the word every day. We must remember that what we have received as a gift, we must give as a gift, and that all we do should be for the glory of God.

Week Three
Prayerful Reflection

My Children,

You have read the four written gospels. I am asking you to be the fifth gospel – the unwritten gospel. I am asking you to go forth and announce the Good News to all. "How beautiful are the feet of those who bring Good News!" But how can others believe the Good News if they have not heard, and how can they hear if they have not been taught, and how can they be taught if you are not sent out?

You are my fifth gospel. I am sending you. Go forth and announce the Good News to all. The harvest is great, but the workers are few.

Thank you for the many ways you serve me. I love you!.

Week Four
Inspired Thought

United in One Body

And let the peace of Christ rule in your hearts
to which you were called in the One Body.
(Colossians 3:15)

Although the Good News is preached in many languages, they who serve God speak the same language united in one body, with Christ as the head. There are no divisions that separate us from God or each other.

As Christians, we must welcome all to our meetings and resist the urge to look upon anyone with favor or disfavor, for judging others encourages dissent and is unwholesome. Jesus told us in Matthew 7:1-4: "Stop judging that you may not be judged; look not at the splinter in your brother's eye unless you have removed the log in your own eye." Paul tells us in 2 Timothy 2:20: "In a large house there are vessels not only of gold and silver, but also of wood and earthenware. Some are for special use and others for common use." Each of us, though different, has a role.

Let us avoid the tendency to complain unjustly. Granted not all complaints are displeasing to the Lord. God did not ignore the cry of complaint about Sodom and Gomorrah and he destroyed those wicked cities. Also, in Jerusalem, complaints arose on behalf of the widows who were being overlooked and consequently the situation was corrected. Let us open our ears to legitimate complaints. Let us pray for discernment to distinguish between the valid complaints and the ones which stem from jealousy and division. We are called to serve the Lord in an impartial and non-judgmental manner, avoiding gossip and realizing that we need one another.

Let us respect and appreciate the individual personality of each and every person that attends our prayer meeting. They too, have been wonderfully created in the image of God. Our meetings are the vehicle that God has chosen for us to render the noble service of spreading his Good News, and we must not disappoint him. St. Paul tells us in 1 Corinthians 9: 19-22: "I have made myself all things to all men in order to save at least some of them. In fact, I do all that I do for the sake of the gospel in the hope of having a share in its blessings."

We are part of a prayer community which is a gift from God. We must never take what we have for granted. Let us prayerfully protect this precious gift. We heard the Lord call our name and we responded. For this he has rewarded us and we praise him for his blessings on our group, blessings which are pressed down, shaken together and overflowing. Paul tells us in Hebrews 10: 24-25: "We must consider how to rouse each other to love and perform good works. We should not absent ourselves from the assembly as some do, but encourage one another." It is crucial that we are faithful in attending our assembly, our prayer meeting. Every member's participation is indispensable in that we never know when the Holy Spirit will use one of us to encourage someone in need. So let us welcome everyone who enters our prayer community and shower upon them the love that Christ has generously bestowed on each one of us.

Week Four
Prayerful Reflection

My Children,

You have a special mission. Your prayer group is very valuable to me. It is a tool that I will use to spread my word. Do not underestimate its importance. If it continues to be used for the purpose I intended, it will be fruitful and many souls will be saved. If it is of my word and me, it will last; if not, it will fade and disappear.

I rejoice in the celebration of your yearly anniversaries. These past years many of your friends who have died entered into my kingdom because their faith and belief was strengthened through your prayer community. I have called each of you to do a particular work. It is your own work and no one else can do it for you. There are lost souls I have put in your path that you alone are to save. Never disregard any of my children who approach you. Some are lost sheep, and you must shepherd them back to the fold. They are your responsibility.

Before you can do this, you must learn to be all things to my people. Never show partiality – thinking one person more important than another. Always remember to love the sinner and not the sinfulness. You are all part of my one body, but I have given you each special talents since you each have your own individual work to do. These gifts which I have given you are to be used to save souls.

Our relationship must be based on trust and friendship. I cherish your friendship. No greater love is there than to lay down one's life for a friend. When you want your friends to do something, you let them know. If your friends do not understand, you repeat it. Finally, if they still do not comprehend, you take them by the hand and patiently show them. So it is with me. If you do not understand my will, I will gently take you by the hand, revealing all you need to know.

Never forget, I am a merciful God. Pray deeply and I will fill you with discernment. You and I will work together to save souls. All I desire from you is that you dedicate your heart, hands and time to me. You must love all, but be wise and cautious. Be cunning for the evil one will try to trip you up because he will want you to fail. Do not be discouraged. I am with you. Surround yourself with the power of my Holy Spirit.

May the blessing of many more anniversaries be upon you. Shalom, my friends.

Week Five
Inspired Thought

Shedding our Skin in Order to Grow

Bear with each other and forgive whatever grievances you may have against one another. Forgive as the Lord forgave you.
(Colossians 3:13)

I recently read an article about a woman named Kathy Dempsey. She had been a nurse for many years. In 1986, it was not mandatory for health care workers to wear gloves. Kathy pricked her finger while treating a patient who was HIV positive. She contracted the disease. Consequently, her whole life fell apart. Kathy lost her job and many friends shunned her. In despair, she thought of suicide. Miraculously, three months after her initial diagnosis, she inexplicably tested negative. Kathy had the opportunity to start over but was not able to do so because she was holding on to past grievances.

During this devastating period in her life, Kathy found herself consoling a friend who was told by a veterinarian that her pet lizard was dying. Reptiles are creatures that must shed their skin annually in order to allow new skin to form. On rare occasions, a lizard does not shed its skin which results in the lizard's suffocating itself to death. After listening to the story of what happened to the lizard, Kathy was able to apply this same situation to herself. As a result, she was inspired to begin an organization called "Keep Shedding." Kathy became a motivational speaker and author. As a symbol of inspiration for her audience, a 10 inch plastic lizard accompanies her wherever she appears.

I too, was inspired by the story of the lizard and decided to look up the word "shed" in the dictionary. The definition is: to discard, to throw away or to get rid of. How often do we hold on to painful memories that hold us in limbo and prevent us from growing! We read how important it is for us to discard clothing we no longer wear, to empty closets of articles we no longer use, and we are told that "less is more." Yet it is more important to rid ourselves of the excess baggage that invades our mental, emotional and spiritual health. Why do we keep on living in the past – harboring unpleasant memories, replaying painful experiences and focusing on hurtful images? We need to learn to "Let go and let God!" If we do not shed these encumbrances, we too will suffocate. We cannot grow! We cannot go forth!

Each spring my husband starts his garden by planting flower seeds. Every day he faithfully waters them. Some seeds do not take root. These are the seeds that remain whole. They do not shed their skins. They do not grow. Jesus enlightens us in John 12:24: "I solemnly assure you, unless the grain of wheat dies, it remains just a grain of wheat. But if it dies, it produces much fruit."

It is crucial for us to take inventory of all the negativities we harbor and the thoughts that prevent us from developing into the people we should be. What a waste of time and precious energy; time and energy that can be used positively to serve others! Forgiveness plays such an important part in our being able to shed what is unholy and unhealthy. We must pray every day to God, "Forgive us our trespasses as we forgive those who have trespassed against us."

What a wonderful and magnificent God we serve! He teaches us his ways through the breaking of the bread, through his sacraments, through his word, and even through a little pet lizard. All we have to do is open our eyes and we will see him, open our ears and we will hear him, and open our hearts and we will feel his presence!

Week Five
Prayerful Reflection

My Children,

I told you that I would never abandon you. I have kept my word by sending you the Holy Spirit, who is always present to you. The Spirit will rest upon you. It is the Spirit of wisdom and truth, the Spirit of knowledge and of power. The Spirit will provide you with the fruits and gifts you need to do my holy will. The Spirit will instill in you a loving and patient heart. The Spirit will help you to look graciously and kindly on others. The Spirit will help you to be compassionate and understanding, without unjust criticism, when you look upon the faults of others. The Spirit will give you the perseverance to bear up under weariness, strain and persecution. Do you wish to grow spiritually and draw closer to me? Only through the power of the Spirit will you be able to accomplish this. Remember, you have not received the spirit of the world but the Spirit of God. This has been given to you in order that you may understand my teachings.

As you serve and reveal my word to others, do not be anxious or afraid for the Spirit will impart to you my peace, a peace which transcends all human understanding. Depend on the Spirit to give you discernment.

Learn from the Holy Spirit when you feel stifled and are spiritually at a roadblock. Seek the Holy Spirit to heal and comfort you when you are troubled.

Let your pleas pierce the heavens and I will hear them. Pray often: "My Lord bless me and keep me. Make your face shine upon me and be gracious to me. Lord, lift up your countenance to me and give me your peace. Amen."

Week Six
Inspired Thought

For Your Extra Added Enjoyment!

What does man gain by all the toil at which he toils under the sun?
A generation goes, and a generation comes, but the earth remains forever.
(Ecclesiastes 1:3)

A woman and I traveling on the same train started up a conversation, and as we were speeding along, I made a comment about the many hundreds of beef cattle visible from the window. "We sure live in a prosperous country," I remarked. She commented, "Somehow cattle don't thrill me. What caught my eye are those little daisies growing in the far corner of the meadow. There is more hope for humanity in a wild flower than there is in a ton of beef." Long after we parted, I kept thinking about her remark. Her point of view, of course, was that a wild flower is one of life's extras that God gives us, one of those things that we do not necessarily need to exist, but we enjoy all the more for that reason.

God's creation supplies us with necessities and extras. Sunlight, air, water, food and shelter – these are necessities. We need them to exist, but moonlight, starlight, music, perfume and flowers – these are definite extras. God gives us extras because he not only wants us to survive, he wants us to be happy. To our bodies, he ministers the necessities; to our spirits, he imparts the splendor that adorns creation. It is in a sunset that he fills our hearts with a sense of beauty and awe. It is in a wild flower, exquisitely designed by him, that he gives us a sense of wonder and enjoyment. Look at the color of the sky or the ocean on a clear day. They are sapphire blue. And much of the earth's surface is green. It is not by mere chance that God chose those colors of blue and green to adorn the planet on which we live. Even scientists have concluded that the two most dominant colors which give us an aura of peace and serenity are blue and green. Is it not true that God has enfolded us in a blanket of his love, peace and security? The woman's casual remark about "more humanity in a wild flower" was to be confirmed to me in the days ahead.

I went to visit a dear friend who was very ill. There was a full moon that night and as I walked down the street on my sad mission, its silvery glow quieted my heart with enormous peace. I had this tremendous feeling that God was saying to me, "Look at the beauty of the night. Enjoy this perfect night! Bathe yourself in its splendor and it will take away your sadness."

When I finally reached my friend's house, I found him in bed facing the open window. He, too, was aware of the moonlight shining on the trees, and the special glow it cast over the neighborhood. He felt the breeze coming in from the open window and breathed in the perfume from the flowers in his garden. As I sat beside him, a mockingbird began chanting divinely and his song touched our spirits. We did not speak. There was no need. We felt the love and peace in the air which permeated our souls.

On the table by his bed, were all the necessities needed for a sick man (cough medicine, inhalers, antibiotics, etc.), but he received small comfort from them. However, the moonlight, the fragrance of the flowers, the wild song of the bird, all the extras that God has given us, these are what brought peace to his heart. Quietly, we sat together for the longest time, enjoying the extras that God had blessed us with that summer night.

Long after he had recovered, we met again and he said to me, "Do you remember the night you came to visit me? I didn't think I was going to make it, but the moment I heard the bird sing and saw the moonlight, I knew I would get well. I felt all the peace and beauty of that night, and I knew God was trying to show us how much he loved us. That night God did not speak words, but instead showed me his love by giving me everything I needed to get well—not only the necessities, but the extras!"

Week Six
Prayerful Reflection

My Children,

Come! Let us celebrate together in this holy place. You have come into my Father's house where there is joy! Let there be song. With sanctified hearts lift your voices and hands in praise and thanksgiving. Feel the brush of angel's wings as they join you. Blast the trumpets and sound the cymbals. My Holy Spirit will set your feet-a-dancing, and the joy of this night will set your hearts-a-singing.

I embrace you for all your good works. Let every living creature that has breath give praise. This is a night of joy! Cherish this moment you are spending with me. I created this moment just for you and me. I know how difficult it is for you to be still, to focus on being with me rather than doing for me. You are always in a hurry, but I am not. Tonight is a celebration of all our memories together. Give thanks for all the friendships you have made, for all those friends who have gone on before you, and for all the years we have bonded together. Be steadfast and faithful, and my Holy Spirit will pour out many blessings on your prayer community, and it will continue to thrive. You cannot imagine how much pleasure I receive from being in your company, and I miss you when you are far from me.

Taste and see the goodness I have prepared for you! I have created this moment in time just for you and me. Rejoice and be glad in it!

Week Seven
Inspired Thought

Live in His Presence

In him was life and the life was the light of all people.
The light shines in the darkness, and the darkness did not overcome it.
(John 1:4)

When you are exhausted, frustrated, overwhelmed, or run down, your body is saying that you are doing things that are none of your business. God does not require from you what is beyond your ability, or what makes you depressed or sad. Restore yourself by resting in our Lord. He alone can replenish your spirit in order to meet your daily tasks.

God wants you to live in his presence and to bring his presence to others. At times, serving God requires that you go through periods of suffering, tiredness, and even moments of great physical or emotional pain. Often times, the hardest pain to bear is your own, but if you take up your cross willingly, God will use your pain to reveal to others their own way to joy, peace and freedom. This is one of the ways we are called to give witness to the faith we have in him that "all things work to the good."

Remember the words from Romans 8: 35: "Who shall separate us from the love of Christ? Shall trouble or hardship or persecution or danger or sword? We are more than conquerors through him who loved us." Nothing must ever separate you from the love of God, because it is only through him that you can serve others to the fullest.

Mother Teresa always started the day by immersing herself in deep prayer. Before she could even begin to get involved with the day's hectic activities, she needed to soak herself in therapeutic prayer time. She strictly adhered to the words, "Your will be done, not mine," and so must we. It is not easy to give your agenda to God, but the more you do so, the more you will realize that your "clock time" becomes "God's time," and "God's time," is always the "fullness of time."

Each of us, in our own individual way, must use the gifts that God has given us to serve others. We must sit at the Lord's feet and listen to him speak to our heart. We must share these words of knowledge with others. His words will be manna from heaven to all those we meet.

You are on a journey and sometimes you do not know where the road you are on will take you. Hopefully, it will draw you closer to the Lord. There are times when you doubt, and you say to yourself, "It isn't going to work. My journey towards spirituality is at an end." It is hard not to listen to these words of self-doubt, but do not heed them. Know that this is not God's voice. Listen to God as he speaks to you. "I love you. I am with you. I want to see you come closer to me and experience the joy and peace of my presence in your life. I want to give you a new heart and a new spirit. I want you to speak with my mouth, see with my eyes, hear with my ears and touch with my hands. All that is mine is yours. Just trust me and let me be your God."

Week Seven
Prayerful Reflection

My Children,

If you just touch the hem of my garment, you shall be healed. I am among you, but you are only aware of the crowd. You do not see me. Others block your vision of me. Look for me. Search me out. I am never far from you. Touch my cloak and I will heal you. I wish to make of you what pleases me. You have a special calling to serve me. Each child of mine is valuable and precious in my sight, but I cannot use you to the fullness of your ability when you are preoccupied with personal problems. Whoever puts his hand to the plow, but keeps looking back, is unfit for the reign of God.

I know you are afraid and insecure, but you must learn to trust me. Touch my garment and hold on, and I will give you courage that is not of this world. This is the revelation my saints understood. No matter how heavy their cross, no matter what they had to endure, they were never afraid.

I am building an army of soldiers because there will be difficult times ahead. Fear will be useless; what is needed is trust. Always envision yourself holding on tightly to my garment. In this manner you will realize that I am always with you to guide and instruct you in my ways, and you will be amazed at what I will accomplish through you. My garment is a mantle that will cover and protect you from any evil that might attack you. Do not be discouraged. My victory over sin is for all who believe I am the resurrection and the life. They who believe in me will have eternal life.

"All flesh is as grass, and their glory is like the flowers of the field: the grass withers and the flowers fall, but the word of the Lord endures forever." (1 Peter 1: 24-25)

Week Eight
Inspired Thought

Our Blessed Mother Speaks

At the wedding in Cana, Mary said, "Do whatever he tells you!
(John 2:5)

I was praying to the Blessed Mother statue, and these words came to mind: 'You are praying to a block of stone; yet because of your faith, you speak to me as if I were really listening to you. Because of your belief, you have taken this block of stone and turned it into flesh. I have become real to you. Let this be a lesson to you. When people appear to be harsh, cold and act as if they were blocks of stone, talk to them as you talk to me. Their hearts of stone will become hearts of flesh. When your own heart has hardened and you cannot forgive, think of my Son who had no one to comfort him on his walk to Calvary. His heart never hardened towards anyone. It was a heart filled with mercy. His was a heart of flesh. If you think on these things, the hardness in your own heart will melt with pity and compassion towards those who treat you unjustly and hurt you.'

I truly felt that Mary was inspiring me to learn an important lesson as I knelt before her statue. There is much anger in the world today towards those who have committed horrendous acts of terror, and even though this may be justified, anger and hatred never solved a problem. In all parts of the world brother is fighting against brother. Their hearts have turned to stone. There is no reasoning.

It is important that we pray for the perpetrator as well as the victim. The Father's mercy is for all. His mercy is for the just and the unjust. The commandment to love your enemy is not just empty words, but the key to peace in the world and in our hearts. The Father's mercy endures forever and so should ours.

Week Eight
Prayerful Reflection

My Children,

I am love and I want to take up residence in your heart. You must never let evil enter into your heart, because if you do, it will make a home there. Love and hate cannot live in the same heart.

You must love and strive to be holy. Your Blessed Mother is an example of what holiness is. I have asked her to watch over all my children, and she has once again obediently said. "Yes!" Pray to her. She will teach you how to rid yourself of all that is sinful in your life. Listen! She will touch your heart with inspiration and guide you spiritually on the right path. She is a wise and generous mother, who loves greatly and wants only what is best for all of humanity.

The evil one is cunning. You must always be on guard. Do not allow others to lead you into sin. Hating others will turn your hearts to stone. Those who say, "I love God, but hate my brother or sister," are liars.

Those who do not love a brother or sister whom they have seen cannot love God whom they have not seen. Whoever says, "I am in the light," while hating a brother or sister is still in darkness. Those who do not love abide in death.

I command you to love one another as I have loved you. Your love for me does not diminish when you love others, it will increase. This is because it is the wish of the Father that the love he has bestowed on his Son, is also bestowed on all of humanity, so that we may all be one!

Week Nine

Inspired Thought

You Never Learn Anything by Talking

My sheep hear my voice. I know them, and they follow me.
(John 10:27)

Larry King is a talk show host known for his skill at interviewing guests. Once asked what the best words of advice anyone ever gave him were, he responded: "You never learn anything by talking." When King feels himself talking more than the person he is interviewing, he remembers to be still and let his guest talk. It is his guests that the viewers are interested in learning more about; Larry is there only to facilitate the process.

In Luke 10: 38, we learn that a woman named Mary knew the value of listening. Jesus spoke the words of life and Mary listened and learned. She knew when to quit serving and when to start listening. Mary had chosen the better portion and it was not to be taken from her. Know God – Know peace. No God – No peace. Mary had her mind set on that which comes from above and not on worldly things. Mary is a definite model for our hurricane lifestyle. Visualize Mary sitting, listening, and worshiping at the Lord's feet. Mary wanted to learn. She was hungry for the word and she discovered that by sitting at our Lord's feet and listening quietly, he would teach her.

Week Nine
Prayerful Reflection

My Children,

I want you to be a listener. No one seems to have the time to listen to others. You do not even listen to those who love you. I want you not only to listen to their words, but to listen to what is not being said, to be aware of their body language. I want you to slow down and take the time to listen intensely, concentrating fully on what is being said to you. Concentrate on what someone is telling you. Remove all other thoughts from your mind. The lack of a sympathetic ear is one of the tragic truths of modern life. A human's most important need is for someone to listen to them as they reveal their innermost thoughts.

I wish for you to discern when you must be silent. You will be a comfort to others if you allow them to speak to you. Listening to their problems will be a source of healing for them. There are so many of my children who are in pain because they have no one to listen to them unburden their thoughts. Remember, you must listen in confidence, and then remain silent about what they have told you.

Learn from me. I wish to teach you. I am the listener. Whether you are friend or foe, man, woman or child, happy or sad, well or ill, I am with you, waiting for you to talk to me. I listen earnestly to all you have to say. I never grow tired of having you talk to me. I behold you in your nakedness, in your wounds, in your secret grief, in your despair, in your betrayals, and in your pain. I listen to your unexpressed thoughts and sorrows. I listen to your heart when terror strikes. I listen as your tears fall when you are abandoned. I listen for a moment, an hour, a day, a lifetime!

Because I am silent, you think I am not present. I hear you say, "O God is there no one to listen?" You ask, "Is there no one to listen?" Yes! I am the one who listens, who will always listen. Hasten to me. Come! Tell me everything, my friend. I am listening!

Week Ten

Inspired Thought

The Holy Spirit – My Muse

You are the light of the world!
(Matthew. 5:14)

I saw a movie called The Muse. It taught me an important lesson because it shows how God speaks to us through various means. A muse is a mythological female creature that inspires creativity. During a dry spell, she helps writers, composers and artists to create. She not only inspires, but instills in them a boldness to forge ahead – to share with others the gifts they have received. The results may bring recognition, money, and fame to the person. The muse does not do the creating. She inspires the person who calls on her to create. In return, the person generally bestows gifts of all sorts on the muse.

We have a muse. It is the Holy Spirit who fills us with creative gifts and inspirational thoughts. How are we to pay back this muse? By sharing with others what he has inspired in us. This, along with praise and thanks, is the only payback the Holy Spirit expects from us. We celebrate the feast of Pentecost, the coming of the Holy Spirit upon the Apostles, which is the beginning of the Church. If it were not for the Holy Spirit, the church would not exist as we know it today and the Charismatic Movement would not have begun. We must ask for and use the gifts of the Holy Spirit to continue to build up the Body of Christ. Only then can we bear fruit and be a light to the world; a beacon to others in darkness.

Just before Lent begins, our prayer group celebrates Fat Tuesday. It is a day when we all get together as a community to share a hearty meal and good conversation. On one of these occasions, I had a tremendous feeling that God was surrounding us with his light and calling each one of us to be a beacon. At our meeting the following Wednesday, there was a prophecy confirming my feelings that we are all being called to be beacons for others. A beacon serves as a signal for those that are lost; a light in the darkness; a guide to help them find their way. In Matthew 5:15, Jesus explains: "Men do not light a lamp and then put it under a bushel basket. They set it on a stand where it gives light to all in the house." A beacon is placed very high on a lighthouse. It is a guide to ships that are lost or in trouble. Its purpose is to deliver them from perishing in the darkness.

Let us then become a beacon to those around us; not a flickering light, but a bright, piercing beacon. Let us do away with all negativity and light up our surroundings in order that we may help others who are in darkness. And let us always allow the muse of the Holy Spirit to inspire us, so that we may use his gifts to become the light that will guide others to draw closer to God and prevent them from perishing in the darkness.

Week Ten
Prayerful Reflection

My Children,

I want you to light up the world. Become one candle burning in the darkness, giving light to others. Your light will be like a blazing fire that warms the coldness of those around you. Like a candle, you will melt in service to others. As the shape of the candle changes when it burns, I will mold you and fashion you to your fullest potential.

Let your love for others burn with a fervor that will render itself to all those you meet. Let your being radiate an incense that will soften the hardest of hearts.

"What light can come from a little candle?" you might ask. Don't you remember the last blackout? At that time you and all your neighbors lit candles when the electricity failed. What a comfort the light from those candles brought to everyone! This is all I ask of you: "Be a little candle, a little light, and comfort my people. Then, you will start a blaze for all those in darkness, and no one or nothing will quench it."

Week Eleven

Inspired Thought

Called to Be a Witness

All scripture is inspired by God
and is useful for teaching, for rebuking, for correction,
and for training in righteousness so that everyone who belongs to God
may be thoroughly equipped for every good work.
(Timothy 3:16)

We are called to be witnesses. We are commanded to go forth and spread the Good News. In John 17:20 Jesus said: "I pray for those you gave me (those who believe), but I also pray for those who will come to believe in me."

In the parable of "The Prodigal Son" (Matthew 21:28) Jesus tells the story of the faithful son who stayed with his father. This son was obedient and did what his father asked. He was one with his father. We also learn about the unfaithful son who left his father to squander his inheritance and enjoy the pleasures that the world had to offer. The unfaithful son filled with repentance, eventually returns. Jesus continues to explain how the father rejoiced when his son returned, "My son was dead, but has now come back to life!"

I have often wondered what really made the son return. We know from reading this scripture that the son had wasted all his money, was starving and homeless. But was there another reason? Did someone witness to him? Did someone take the time to show him the error of his ways? What finally made him truly repent and ask to be forgiven? What finally made him come to his senses? The father is so overjoyed to have this son back, he cries out: "He was lost, but is now found. This is cause to rejoice and celebrate."

In John 10:11, Jesus tells us: "I am the good shepherd. I know my sheep and my sheep know me." The sheep that know him and hear his voice are the faithful ones. But Jesus also says: "I have other sheep that do not belong to this fold." These are the lost sheep, the ones that can be compared to the unfaithful son. It is our responsibility to act on what he has commanded us to do, which is to bear witness to those who are lost.

We may be intimidated when we have to witness to someone we know, or members of our own family. Perhaps we are afraid they will make fun of us or not take us seriously; or maybe we are just too plain embarrassed. During petition time, how often have we heard our members lift up their loved ones because they are missing the experience of having a personal relationship with Jesus? If someone we know is going through hard times and needs healing and wholeness but cannot call on their faith to give them the strength and courage they need, it is only because they do not know their savior, Jesus Christ. They cannot cling to him in times of adversity because they do not believe, and maybe the reason for their unbelief is that no one took the time to enlighten them of what Jesus can do in their lives. We who are called to be a light in the darkness may find it easier to speak to strangers than to our own. As a result, we may experience a tremendous feeling of guilt because we did not take the time or were not courageous enough to approach someone close to us and share with them the message of the Good News. Perhaps we are hesitant to approach others because we are concerned that we might be rejected; but it will comfort us to know that Jesus had this same problem. "I came to my own, and my own rejected me. A prophet is not accepted in his own town." The Pharisees jeered at the crowd, "Is this not the carpenter's son?" (Matthew 13: 54-58)

Let nothing or no one deter us from doing God's work. Be confident and have faith that his Holy Spirit will provide us with the words we need when we reach out to those in darkness. Appreciate this gift of faith we have been given. We will be held responsible to share this gift of faith and enlighten those who are in darkness. Much has been given to us through this gift of faith. Let us not forget his words, "To those whom much has been given, much will be required."

The Bible is filled with many references that encourage us to go forth and make disciples of all nations. Here are a few:

> Acts 1:8- "You will receive power when the Holy Spirit comes down on you; then you are to be my witnesses in Jerusalem, throughout Judea and Samaria, yes even to the ends of the Earth." Jesus Christ has been raised up and we are his witnesses.

> John 5:31- John wrote: "That which was from the beginning, which we have heard, which we have seen with our eyes, which we have looked at and our hands have touched, this we proclaim concerning the word of life. The life appeared; we have seen it and testify to it, and we proclaim to you the eternal life, which was with the Father and has appeared to us. We proclaim to you what we have seen and heard, so that you also may have fellowship with us. And our fellowship is with the Father and with His Son, Jesus Christ. This is the message we have heard

from him and declare to you: God is light; in him there is no darkness at all. If we claim to have fellowship with him yet walk in darkness, we lie and do not live by the truth. But if we walk in the light, as he is in the light, we have fellowship with one another, and the blood of Jesus, his Son, purifies us from all sin."

Acts 26:15- Saul asked, "Who are you, Lord?" "I am Jesus, whom you are persecuting," the Lord replied. "Now get up and stand on your feet. I have appeared to you to appoint you to be a servant and a witness as to what you have seen of me and what I will show you. I will rescue you from your own people and from the Gentiles. I am sending you to them to open their eyes and turn them from darkness to light and from the power of Satan to God, so that they may receive forgiveness of sins and a place among those who are sanctified by faith in me."

Acts 13:46- Then Paul and Barnabas answered them boldly: "We had to speak the word of God to you first. Since you rejected it and do not consider yourselves worthy of eternal life, we now turn to the Gentiles. For this is what the Lord has commanded us: "I have made you a light for the Gentiles, that you may bring salvation to the ends of the earth."

2 Corinthians 4:13- It is written: "I believed; therefore, I have spoken. With that same spirit of faith, we also believe and therefore speak, because we know that the one who raised the Lord Jesus from the dead will also raise us with Jesus and present us with you in His presence. All this is for your benefit, so that the grace that is reaching more and more people may cause thanksgiving to overflow to the glory of God. Therefore, do not lose heart. Though outwardly we are wasting away, yet inwardly, we are being renewed day by day; for our light and

momentary troubles are achieving for us an eternal glory that far outweighs them all. So we fix our eyes not on what is seen, but on what is unseen; for what is seen is temporary, but what is unseen is eternal."

Matthew 2:18- And Jesus came and said to them, "All authority in heaven and on earth has been given to me. Go, therefore, and make disciples of all nations, baptizing them in the name of the Father and the Son, and of the Holy Spirit, and teaching them to obey everything that I have commanded you. Remember, I am with you always, to the end of the age."

We need search no farther than the New Testament for all of the inspiration and instruction that we need to help us to become a witness and share the Good News. Jesus is calling us the same way he called to brothers Simon and Andrew (Matthew 4:19) as they were casting their nets into the sea: "Come after me and I will make you fishers of men."

Week Eleven
Prayerful Reflection

My Children,

The Lenten season is once again upon us. It is the time of year when you think of fasting and giving alms and I appreciate your efforts in this regard. But what truly pleases me is when you rend your hearts and not your garments. What I am asking of you is to have a heart filled with compassion and mercy for all those you meet. I know it is not easy to love those who do not love you, those who annoy and vex you, those with whom you do not see eye to eye. At times your heart will be filled with anguish; you will feel as if you are being torn in two. It will take great sacrifice on your part but I have called you to be a light in the world. The significance of these words is that I am sending you to bear witness to me and to save those who are lost. Those in darkness must see a great light – your light! I am the good shepherd. You, my faithful ones, recognize my voice. You must enlighten those who do not know me.

I have heard you struggle in prayer as you lift up members of your family. Do not be discouraged. Remember, that I stand at the right hand of my Father, and intercede for all those you lift up in prayer. My Father will hear your prayers, and at a time that is acceptable to him, salvation will come to those you are lifting up. My Father will not reject any prayer that is offered to save a soul. Do not be discouraged for I myself, was rejected by those who knew me. When all was hopeless and all seemed lost, my Father transformed what appeared to be evil into good.

When you lift your loved ones up in prayer, you must pray for every aspect of their lives. Pray that they may be blessed in health and in work. Pray that they may clearly discern the truth. Pray that they may have wholesome relationships and good attitudes. Pray that they may resist temptation. Let them know that you are praying for them. Most people are comforted by the fact that they are being prayed for, even when they do not believe. Prayers are powerful forces which pierce the throne of heaven. Never give up!

Luke 18:1 tells about a widow's perseverance and the need to pray always and not lose heart: "In that city was a widow who kept coming to the judge asking, 'Grant me justice against my opponent.' For a while he refused, but because the widow kept bothering him, he granted her request. And the Lord said, 'Will not God grant justice to his chosen ones who cry to him day and night? Will he delay in helping them? He will quickly grant justice to them. And yet, when the Son Man comes, will he find faith on Earth?' "

Praying for others opens their hearts to receive a life-changing encounter. I hear your prayers and I am watching over all of my children. My greatest desire is that my lost children come back to me with all their hearts. I want this even more than you want it. You cannot imagine what seeds you are planting through your prayers. Never feel your prayers do not matter. In your prayer of faith, you have shown me that you believe my promise that whatever you pray for in my name, I will answer. Every answered prayer is a miracle, and those who are lost will come to believe in me through your prayers.

Remember, you are my beloved faithful. You are with me always and everything I have is yours. I am preparing a banquet for you and we will have cause to celebrate when the one who is lost is found, and when the one who is dead, comes back to life.

Week Twelve
Inspired Thought

God Experienced Something New on Good Friday

Yea, though I walk through the valley of the shadow of death,
I will fear no evil; for thou art with me.
(Psalm 23:4)

In his humanity, God, who knows all things, who can do all things and who is all powerful, must have felt and experienced fear when he was about to die on the cross. God, who was and is and will always be, became human through his Son Jesus and as Jesus, he experienced what we humans go through at the hour of death. He really and truly became one with us. He experienced fear, pain, shame, embarrassment, abandonment and death itself.

God cannot die, yet through Jesus' humanity, he obeyed the Father's will and entered the valley of death; all this because he loved us and wanted to open the sealed gates of eternity for us.

We are children of God, and what we will be has not yet been made known to us, but we do know that when Jesus appears again, we shall be like him, for we shall see him as he is. (1 John 3:2)

Week Twelve
Prayerful Reflection

My Children,

Tonight I ask you to gaze at the crucifix. All wisdom stems from the reality of the cross. Gaze on me, and I will reveal to you what is hidden from others who do not look at me. I freely accepted my suffering and death on the cross because of the great love I have for all of you. You also must freely accept suffering when it enters your lives, not because of the law, but because of the spirit of the law which is love. The punishment of sin is death, but through the cross I have given you a gift from my Father, the gift of everlasting life. You must go among the people and testify to this truth.

Many of my children still live in darkness. I thirst and my heart is heavily saddened for those who do not know me. I weep for lost souls. All are called by me, but few are worthy to be chosen. I am calling you to be my witnesses to spread the Good News. As my witnesses, you must be above reproach. I place a heavy burden upon you, but sharing the knowledge of the gift of eternal life will help me save souls. I am sending you forth as a light in the darkness. Before the end days, many will preach the Good News of a heavenly kingdom and you too, shall be my witnesses to all the nations.

Week Thirteen
Inspired Thought

Reflections on Padre Pio's "Into the Light"

We must go down into the darkness in order to come up to the light.
(Padre Pio)

I began to reflect on Padre Pio's "Into the Light":

"In the Christian story, Jesus descended into hell. On the third day, he rose again from the dead and ascended into heaven. Jesus descends into darkness, only to ascend into light. One has the picture of a strong man stooping lower and lower to get himself underneath some great complicated burden. He must stoop down in order to lift us up.

In this descent and ascent, everyone will recognize a familiar pattern that occurs all over the world. It is the pattern of all vegetation . . . we place a seed into the dirt, into the darkness in order for the plant, flower or vegetable to ascend into the light. It is the pattern of all animal and human life. The sperm enters into the darkness of the womb and when birth occurs, a new life comes out of the darkness into the light. When we die, our bodies ascend into the darkness of the earth, but our souls ascend into the light of heaven. We must first go down in order to go up."

Even when we experience dark periods in our lives, he is always with us. At these times we might look back and see only one set of footprints and we might ask, "Where is he? Why isn't he by my side?" It is when we are burdened by sickness, loneliness, problems, or uncertainty, when we cannot step out in faith, when we find it difficult to stand on our own two feet, that he lifts us up into his arms and carries us like a father with a beloved child. He comforts us and once again we feel safe. He has taken us from the darkness into his light. "The Lord is my light and my salvation; whom shall I fear?" (Psalm 27: 1)

Week Thirteen
Prayerful Reflection

My Children,

In order to draw closer to me, you must enter a new country. You are still living in the old country since is it familiar and you know its ways. You have spent most of your life there and even though you have not quite found what your heart most desires, you remain very attached to the old country and it has become a part of you.

In order for you to become a new creation, you must leave your former self, and enter the new country where your beloved dwells. This requires detachment from things that have become most precious to you: possessions, success, even affection and praise. You must enter naked and vulnerable. The only thing you need bring with you is trust. Trust is essential if you wish to find what you need in this new country.

Jesus tells us that if we seek first the kingdom of God, all things will be given to us.

These are unusual times. All forms of communication are bombarding you at all levels. There is conflict within you! You sense that nothing but God's love can fulfill your deepest needs, but the pull to other people and worldly possessions remains strong. Yet, you are being called to go towards solitude, prayer and great simplicity. Scheduling time away from your friends, unnecessary work, television and newspapers will become easier when you enter the new country. You are being called to go towards solitude, prayer and great simplicity.

You will find supreme happiness in your new home alone with Jesus, listening as he speaks to you. You will become aware of how close he is to you and how much he loves you. You will know that something totally new and truly unique is happening within you – that something is dying and something is being born.

At the beginning you will feel strange in your new country, but Jesus is there and you can trust that he will show you the path you must follow. You must not lose heart or think that after so many years, you cannot change. Simply enter into the presence of Jesus and ask him to give you a fearless heart. You cannot make yourself different, but Jesus can make of you a new creation with a new mind and a new body. As a citizen of God's country, you will realize the joy that comes with the freedom of being a child of God. Welcome to your new home!

Week Fourteen
Inspired Thought

God Alone Gives the Growth

He who supplies seed to the sower and bread for food
will supply and multiply your seed for sowing
and increase the harvest of your righteousness.
(2 Corinthians 9:10)

A seed can only flourish if it remains in the ground in which it is sown. If you keep digging the seed up to check whether it is growing, it will never bear fruit. Think of yourself as a little seed planted in a rich soil. All you need to do is stay there and trust that the soil contains everything you need to grow. This growth takes place even when you do not feel it. It is God who gives the growth.

If in your spiritual growth, you suddenly seem to lose all you had gained, do not despair. Your growth does not occur in a straight line. You must expect setbacks. Don't say to yourself, "All is lost; I will have to start all over again". This is not true. What you have gained, you have gained. Sometimes little things build up and make you feel at first that you have lost ground, but this is only temporary. It could be fatigue, a seemingly cold remark, someone's inability to hear and understand you, or someone's innocent forgetfulness. These things can make you feel as if you are being rejected, and that you are right back where you started. Instead, try to imagine yourself being pulled off the road for a while. When you return to the road, you return to the place you left off, not to where you started.

For your spiritual growth to develop, you must allow yourself to be held and carried by God. In every situation keep trusting that God is with you on your journey. No one person can fulfill all your needs, but God, out of his great love for you, has given you a community of faithful believers who embrace and hold you up when you become discouraged. It is important to remain in touch with those who know you and love you. Think of these people as holding a lifeline that circles around your waist. Wherever you are, this lifeline is with you. If you remain safely anchored in your community, you will have nothing to fear. Then you will be able to carry your light far and wide.

As God uses each person in your community in a special way, so will you too, be present to others in your special way. You have to know and claim your way. That is why discernment is so important. It will help you decide what to do and what not to do; when to speak and when to remain silent; those to be with and those to avoid.

Always remember that someone planted a seed in you and now it is your responsibility, as a servant of the Lord, to plant seeds in others. And never forget that it is God alone who gives the growth!

Week Fourteen
Prayerful Reflection

My Children,

Come! The winter is past. The flowers appear on the Earth. Nature awakens to life. Beloved, you were once lost, but have now been found. You were once dead, but have now tasted eternal life.

I am the vine and you are the branches, and there is abundant fruit for all. Fill yourselves with love, joy, peace, patience, kindness, goodness, faithfulness, and self-control. My fruits are succulent and satisfying. Taste and see the goodness of the Lord. These fruits are the virtues you will need in serving me.

Allow the power of my Holy Spirit to enter into you this night. My Father is very generous and he has chosen a special gift for each of you. It has been waiting for you since the beginning of time. Claim it. Accept it. You must not be afraid that your task will be too difficult. You are the disciples I wish to use as my witnesses to keep my word alive in those who are to come after you. Live completely in my presence and you will not fail.

My cup runneth over. I have told you all these things so that the joy I have and feel for you may abide in you, and your own joy may be complete.

Week Fifteen

Inspired Thought

Jesus, My Silent Love

Give an ear, O Lord to my prayer; listen to my cry of supplication.
In the day of trouble I call on you, for you will answer me.
(Psalms 86:6)

It seems at times that Jesus is silent. How we long to hear his voice in times of trouble. We need reassurance from him. How comforting it would be to hear him say: "Take courage. It is I. Do not be afraid." Yet there is only silence, the unknown, and misery because Jesus did not answer or give us a sign that he heard our pleas.

The silences of Jesus are as eloquent as his words and may be a sign not of his disapproval, but of his approval and his way of providing a deeper blessing. Psalm 43:5 tells us: "Why are you so downcast, O my soul? I will hope in God and I will still praise him." Let us praise him even in his silence toward us.

I once read a legend of a woman who was having a dream. She saw three women in prayer. As they knelt, the Master drew near. He approached the first woman and bent over her with tenderness and grace. He smiled with radiant love and spoke to her in tones of pure, sweet music. Upon leaving her, he came to the second woman. He placed his hand upon her bowed head and gave her one look of loving approval. He then passed the third woman almost abruptly, without even stopping for a word or a glance. The woman having the dream said to herself, "How greatly he must love the first woman. The second gained his approval, but did not experience the special demonstrations of love he gave to the first. The third woman must have grieved him deeply, for he gave her no word at all, not even a passing glance." She wondered what the third woman had done to have been treated so indifferently.

Jesus came before her and said: "O, woman, how wrongly you have interpreted me! The first kneeling woman needs the full measure of my tenderness and care to keep her feet on my narrow way. She needs my love and help every moment of the day, for without them she would stumble into failure. The second woman has a stronger and deeper faith than the first, and I can count on her to trust me, no matter how things may go or whatever people may do. But the third woman, whom I seemed not to notice, even to neglect, has faith and love of the purest quality. I am training her through quick and drastic ways for my holiest and highest service. She knows me intimately and trusts me so completely that she no longer depends on my voice, my loving glances, or other outward signs to know of my approval. She is not dismayed or discouraged by circumstances I arrange for her to encounter. She trusts me when common sense, reason and every instinct of the natural heart would rebel, knowing that I am preparing her for eternity, and realizing that the understanding of what I do will come later. My love is silent because I love beyond the power of words and beyond the understanding of the human heart. My love is silent so that all may learn to trust me purely and simply."

Jesus will do wonders we have never before experienced if we learn the mystery of his silence. Let us praise him always, even in his silence towards us. If he chooses to be silent towards us, it is only because he knows that our faith and trust in him is strong and this pleases him immensely.

We learn from the gospel reading of Matthew 15:23 that at first Jesus may appear silent, but he is always present and attentive: It happened that a Canaanite woman cried out to Jesus, "Lord, Son of David, have pity on me. My daughter is terribly troubled by a demon." *He gave her no word of response.* His disciples began to entreat him, "Get rid of her. She keeps shouting after us." Jesus said to the woman, "My mission is to the House of Israel. It is not right to take the food of sons and daughters and throw it to the dogs." But the woman insisted, "Please Lord, even the dogs eat the leftovers that fall from the master's table." Jesus said in reply, "Woman, you have great faith. Your wish will come to pass." That moment her daughter got better.

The Lord expects from us the same faith, perseverance, and trust that the Canaanite woman had.

Week Fifteen
Prayerful Reflection

My Children,

Why do you act as if I don't exist? I AM. I sent my Son to give witness to you so that you might believe. If you truly believe I AM, you would not let worldly cares interfere with your peace of mind. Why are you disturbed? Why do you take things that happen to you so seriously? Everything on earth is temporary. Set your heart on the place I have prepared for you. It is a place of holiness, well-being, serenity, and joy.

If you truly believe I exist, you would be experiencing this heaven on Earth. Outside influences would not cause you to worry or be afraid.

My saints know this. Because they feel my presence at their side, their burdens become less frightening. "Be not afraid for I am with you," is a saint's creed. My holy ones truly believe that I AM and they act accordingly. My saints face hardship, persecution, servitude, and even death without fear.

I am your courage, strength and protection against the storms of your life. If at times your faith is weak, act as if you have faith and faith will be given to you. I know the world demands much from you. Remember, I too, experienced humanity. I myself tasted the pains, sorrows, disappointments, and betrayals that life thrusts upon you.

You are all my beloved, and my heart is the first to feel the pain and anguish which you are suffering. I am one with each of you, and know your innermost fears and sorrows. Believe I AM and you will be able to withstand all the hardships that come your way. You will never be afraid again.

Share this gift of courage with others. You cannot contain me and keep me for yourselves, as I am for all. I am enlightening you to go forth and instill in my people the courage they will need to face the coming tribulations. Help them to understand they need not fear for I am with them always, even until the end. I am calling you to make a difference in their lives. Do not be afraid to approach others to share my message of faith and courage.

I have created you for a purpose. You are not meant to grow as weeds which are discarded with no trace of their existence. You are everlasting. Any service you provide for one of mine, no matter how small or insignificant you may think it is, will not go unnoticed by me, and you will be rewarded. If on your journey through life, you can take the fear from someone and give them the courage they need to face whatever life has in store, then your living shall not be in vain.

Week Sixteen
Inspired Thought

Heartbeat

*Come to me, all you who are weary and burdened
and I will give you rest.
(Matthew 11:28)*

Heartbeat: the steady pulse of the heart, day and night, never failing. Like the air, it is another thing that we are not conscious of. It does what it is supposed to do to keep us alive.

What patience the heart has to keep its daily rhythm regardless of the abuse we shower on it! Does it come from eating improperly or drinking or smoking too much? Even though our blood pressure is too high and we are filled with anger, anxiety and worry, our heart beats patiently on.

But the heart is a very wise organ. It restores its energy in a very specific way. In between each heartbeat is a rest. The heart rests and there is peace. The heart stops and is quiet for a second - just for a second - but that second helps it to rejuvenate itself.

Imagine the benefit to our bodies, emotions and spirit, if we were to take time out of our hectic lives to be quiet and peaceful even for just a few moments each day; it would change our lives.

We must listen to our heartbeat. It has a very important lesson to teach us.

Week Sixteen
Prayerful Reflection

My Children,

A life that is planned is a closed life. It can be endured, but not lived. I want your life to be filled with joy!

Rid yourself of the tensions that surround you. Rid yourself of schedules that cause you to become anxious. No matter how much you do, no matter how much you accomplish, your chores will never finish. Do not live each day racing to get work done so that you may have time for yourself. You have heard the saying, "Do not put off until tomorrow what you can do today." I tell you for your own good, "Put it off!"

Happiness is not a station in life that automatically arrives at the end of a journey. It should be an important part of your daily life. You must make the time every day to do what gives you pleasure. How sad it is to hear my children say, "I will have time to enjoy that tomorrow, or I'll do that when I retire." You never know when your life will be required of you, and then it will be too late.

I no longer call you my servant. You are my friend and friends must take the time to enjoy each other's company. You were created not only to work, but also to enjoy life! Do not make yourself a slave to always being on time. Do not become annoyed when you are interrupted from a task you are doing. I sometimes send these interruptions to give you a rest period. It is the unexpected surprises in life that you remember and which give you the most enjoyment.

There is a miracle waiting for you in every new day. You have been given this new day to use as you will. It is important that you take the time to enjoy this new day because you are exchanging a day of your life for it. You will never see this day again so ask yourself, "Did I enjoy today?"

When you look back on your life, it will be the things that you neglected to do that you will regret, such as taking the time to look and enjoy the wonders of my creation, enjoying the company of family and friends, or just meditating quietly with a good book in hand. Pray often. Do not be afraid of being silent before me. I will restore you at this time, and you will be refreshed to face the challenges that confront you each day.

What I ask of you is really so simple, and yet so many of you find it difficult to do. Each day, find time to stop your chores and come into my presence and I will fill you with a joy that is not of this world. Once you have experienced this joy, you will understand that there is nothing else quite like it, and spending time with me each day will become for you an awesome experience.

Week Seventeen
Inspired Thought

Lay Down Your Burdens

For my yoke is easy, and my burden is light!
(Matthew 11:30)

I read the story of a tired man who walked along a road, weary and discouraged. He could hardly put one foot in front of the other. A neighbor overtook him and offered him a lift in his wagon. After riding in the wagon for a while, the neighbor noticed the tired weary man still carried the heavy sack of grain on his back. "Put your sack down," said the neighbor. "You don't need to carry that sack. Lay it in the wagon." The tired man said, "Oh, it is enough that you are carrying me. I really appreciate that. You don't have to carry my sack of grain as well."

After I read that story, in my mind I pictured the driver of the wagon to be God telling us to put down our heavy sacks. It is not necessary for us to carry them alone. He offers to help us, but we still carry heavy sacks on our backs. We are anxious and we worry needlessly. We are tired and worn out. We do not enjoy life. We are not free. We do not lay our burdens down. We do not ask for help. God is not going to force us to lay down our burdens. He wants us to believe his words are true and to act upon them. We must take the words of Matthew 11:28 to heart: "Come to me, all you that are weary and are carrying heavy burdens and I will give you rest. Take my yoke upon you, and learn from me; for I am gentle and humble of heart, and you will find rest for your souls, for my yoke is easy, and my burden is light."

But it is not enough for us to hear about placing our burdens in God. It is crucial for us to believe and have the faith that God can, and actually will, relieve us of our burdens. Mark 9:17-27 emphasizes how important our faith is: A man in the crowd said to Jesus, "Teacher, I have brought you my son who is possessed by an evil spirit that has robbed him of his speech. I asked your disciples to drive out the demon, but they could not." Jesus said to his disciples, "*Oh, what tiny faith you have. How much longer must I be with you until you believe?* How much longer must I be patient with you? Bring the boy to me." The father said, "Have mercy on us and do something if you can." "*If I can?*" Jesus answered. "*Everything is possible for him who believes.*" The father instantly replied, "I do believe, help me to overcome my unbelief." So they brought the boy to him. Jesus commanded the spirit to come out of the boy and never enter again. Jesus took the boy by the hand and lifted him to his feet, and he was healed.

If even his own disciples, those that walked the Earth with Jesus, knew him and watched him perform miracles, struggled at times with their faith, how much more difficult it would seem for us! But this too is a burden we can place on his shoulders. Let us pray like the boy's father: "I do believe Lord, but help me overcome my unbelief." Our burdens are lighter when we come to have the faith to believe that through the power of Christ, all things are possible.

Week Seventeen
Prayerful Reflection

My Children,

My work does not begin with work. My work begins with stillness before me in order to produce power and performance. Work that does not begin with resting in me is done without my approval or participation.

Life's work is confusing – people screaming your name and pulling you in all directions. A false sense of duty has put strings on your hands and made a puppet out of you, and the temptation is for you to move quickly. You have much to do! Everything is a crisis! Hurry! You must perform the job that is waiting as you are the only one who can do it. Time seems inadequate to complete the tasks before you.

Resting in me is the first step of work. It begins with stillness before me. My last words on the cross were, "It is finished." In that divine statement, the entire human dilemma was solved, and sin and death were defeated. But these were not the only two problems conquered.

There was also the problem of life, and life is made up of work. The human problem of work was solved in the most amazing way. By resting in me, you trust me to perform the work myself. I will do the work and you will rest. This is your Sabbath rest. Simply come before me and cease striving.

Unburden yourself to me before you try to tackle your daily chores. Take off the human load you carry and lay it on my divine shoulders. We will share the divine yoke. Come to me! Let me sort through the maze of demands and worries. You will discern the tasks which I will for you and eliminate the unnecessary chores and strife in your life.

Resting in me is the place where you must live and to which you must return every day. Do not strive to undertake any task until you have rested in me. Refuse to be part of the human puppet madness. Keep your will fixed on me, and peace will enter your whole being. You have nothing to give to me until you first rest in me and allow me to fill you with myself.

"Those who wait for the Lord shall renew their strength. They shall mount up with wings like eagles. They shall run and not be weary. They shall walk and not faint." (Isaiah 40:31)

Week Eighteen
Inspired Thought

Lessons from a VCR – Buttons on the Remote

But truly it is the spirit in a mortal, the breath of the Almighty
that makes for understanding.
(Job 32:8)

If we are open to the Holy Spirit's inspirations, we can even learn from the remote control of the TV set. This thought came about while I was studying my remote control one day. After this experience, I could never look at the remote in the same way again.

Power – It is the On and Off switch which reminds us that all power comes from on high. We must never be disconnected from God. It is through his power that all things are made possible for us.

Search – Do we search for the wrong things to make us happy? We search, but are never satisfied. "I searched in all the wrong places. I was looking outward, but you were within." (St. Augustine). Let us search for things which are of him and him alone.

Channel – Are we channeled? Do we set goals? Are we focused on him? Is anything interfering with our reception of God's word? Do we hear him loud and clear?

Enter – Do we take the time to enter into the presence of the Lord? Let us learn to live by these words, "Through him, with him and in him."

Volume – Are we surrounded by loud noise? Do we do all the talking? We must lower the volume of the world in order to hear him. Are we timid? When we proclaim his word, do we speak too low or not clearly enough?

Mute – Are we silent before him? Can we hear him as he speaks to us? Are we still before him and know that he is God?

Record – Our minds are like tape recorders which copy everything we see and hear. Are we recording the same thing over and over again? Do we remember to empty the clutter in the recycle bin?

Rewind – Do we have a habit of rewinding to events of the past? Do we keep regretting what we did or failed to do? Are we reliving our past lives constantly? Not only is this not healthy, but it is also a waste of time. And this changes nothing.

Fast Forward – Are we apprehensive of the future? Do we speed through life always anxious and worrying about what tomorrow might bring?

Pause – Do we take the time to reflect on the moment? Do we pause from our chores and enjoy the beauty of God's creation? Do we savor being in the present moment?

Erase – Are we eliminating worry, strife, and episodes of disturbances from the past? Have we learned that it is necessary for us to forgive, but just as important to forget? Are we able to erase the painful remembrances of those who hurt us?

<u>Stop</u> – Do we take the time to stop and smell the flowers? Do we stop and make sure our decisions in life do not separate us from God?

<u>Tuner</u> – Is our aerial connected to the Lord? Is his picture coming in nice and clear? Can we hear his voice without static? Do we have to fine tune him in?

<u>Timer</u> – Do we realize that busyness is not necessarily blessedness? Do we get upset if we cannot keep our schedules? Do we understand that our time is not God's time and that he is always on time? Are we flexible? Can we be spontaneous if the situation demands it? If not, we might miss out on the most rewarding experiences that life has to offer because things that occur unexpectedly can be most memorable and enjoyable.

Week Eighteen
Prayerful Reflection

My Children,

Have you ever wished you could start over? Do you wish you could erase your past mistakes and start with a clean slate? How many times have you said to yourself, "If only. . .?"

I tell you the former things have passed away. They are finished! You cannot take hold of the future until you let go of the past. You must close the door on yesterday. I am the present. I feel your pain. Cling to me and me alone. Stop gazing at the past. Put your childish ways aside and I will make of you a new creation.

Behold me, and you will be changed. I will heal your brokenness. I will make you whole and you will find the peace you are searching for. As St. Paul has told you in 1 Corinthians 13:11: "When I was a child, I spoke as a child, I thought as a child, I reasoned as a child. When I became an adult, I put an end to childish ways. For now we see in a mirror dimly but then we will see face to face. Now I know only in part; then I will know fully, even as I have been fully known. And now faith, hope and love abide, these three, and the greatest of these is love."

Week Nineteen
Inspired Thought

It Only Takes a Moment!

When he saw the crowds, he had compassion for them,
because they were harassed and helpless, like sheep without a shepherd.
(Matthew 9:36)

I recently read about a kind of therapy which says that when we are stressed or suffering, we should put our hands over our hearts or touch our cheeks as we might touch a child we love and are consoling. By saying these simple words to ourselves, "I understand," all the weaknesses, the mistakes, the harsh words, the disappointments and other wrongs we have committed against God and others are transformed in that one moment.

In that one moment, we are also acknowledging our responsibility to be loving, kind, compassionate and forgiving toward ourselves. We must personally experience these feelings if we are to touch others. This way of showing love for ourselves makes us realize we are important to God.

We are all children of God and he loves us dearly. We can never comprehend the love he has for us. We can hear him speak these words to our hearts when we are suffering or in pain: "I understand!"

And it only takes a moment!

Week Nineteen
Prayerful Reflection

My Children,

Come and see the goodness that is around you. You so preoccupy yourselves with all the negativity in the world that you forget to dwell on what is pleasant.

Why do you complain that the weather is too hot or too cold? I created the four seasons and each one has its own purpose. During the cold weather, you will feel more energetic. During the hot weather, you are meant to slow down and restore your energy. Why do you fight nature?

Why do you become dismayed when you are confronted with family problems? I created family life, and each person has a special role. It is not by accident that you are part of your family. I have placed you there because it is where you can do the most good, and I will work many marvels through you. Families have a very special place in my heart. I created the first family of Adam and Eve and placed them in Paradise. It was a place of beauty and harmony, but even Paradise held a snake. Search for the good in your families and you will find it. I have a purpose for each family and it will be accomplished in my time. Have patience and pray for discernment.

Do not become anxious when you hear rumors of wars and catastrophes. Do not be afraid of those who can destroy your body. Instead, fear those who can lead you into eternal damnation. Do not be afraid. All that occurs on Earth is because I permit it to happen. Every event has a purpose and good will triumph always. You must have great faith to trust me in these matters.

Do not become discouraged when stories of corruption in politics, law enforcement and religious institutions are revealed. Search out those leaders who are moral and incorruptible. Pray for them to shepherd and serve my people honestly and faithfully so that when they come into my kingdom, they will be rewarded with a crown that is imperishable.

Surround yourselves with positive people and positive thoughts. Do not lose heart. Pray! If my people, who are called by my name, will humble themselves to pray, then I will hear their prayers and restore their land and their families. Amen!

Week Twenty
Inspired Thought

Insufficient Funds

Have we not all one Father? Has not God created us?
Why then are we faithless to one another?
(Malachi 2:10)

The Constitution, the Bill of Rights and the Declaration of Independence, are promissory notes to the people of the United States that all are created equal and that each person is entitled to the pursuit of happiness. However, many people were excluded from these rights: minorities, women, and various religious sects because every time they tried to cash their promissory notes, the checks came back marked "insufficient funds." The checks bounced. The struggle was hard and long for many of these promissory notes to become valid, including the right to vote and to receive fair pay for a day's work regardless of one's sex or color.

I started thinking of all the promises we make to God. How many times have we said that we are going to change and how many times have we broken our promises. Our check to God bounces. It comes back marked – "insufficient funds."

In Martin Luther King, Jr.'s "I Have a Dream" speech, he said that in his dream all God's people are free. There is no poverty and no discrimination. Whether you are Catholic, Protestant, Jew or Muslim, white or black, yellow or brown, there shall be only honor and dignity for all of God's children. God invites us all to the mountaintop. However, the Promised Land will not be attained by violence, guns and revenge but by a barrage of love. We will not reach the mountain by how long we live, but by how well we live!"

Week Twenty
Prayerful Reflection

My Children,

You say you know me, but you are far from me. Those who truly know me love all my people unconditionally. There are no exceptions, no excuses. Now you see me imperfectly as looking through a mirror – you see only my reflections. But once you know me, you will come to see and understand my ways perfectly.

You do not know me if you are called to the religious life but do not follow the first commandment to love me with all your heart, mind and soul and to take care of those I have entrusted to you.

You do not know me if you are parents but have ignored your responsibilities to your children and spouse.

You do not know me if you are teachers and do not embrace your vocation to lead your students on the right path.

You do not know me if you are doctors and nurses, and have forsaken your oath to heal the sick and minister to the dying.

You do not know me if you are leaders of government and do not strive for peace instead of war.

How can you say you know and love me when you neglect to extend a helping hand to a neighbor who desperately needs your love and kindness?

To those who have been given much, I expect much and I will hold them accountable for not easing the pain of the least of my brethren. I became human in order to speak to you in words you can understand. You read my words of everlasting life, but many of you do not wish to follow the way of the cross. It is difficult, but with me all things are possible.

What merit is there in loving those who love you? If you can learn to love all people to the same degree without pre-judging or criticizing, your life will be happier and richer. You cannot imagine the joy and peace that will fill your being. This way of life will become a magnificent passion, because then you will be able to honestly say, "I have heard my Master's words. I have been blessed to see him face to face and now I truly know him."

Week Twenty-One
Inspired Thought

The Holy Spirit – The Forgotten Side of God

I will pour out my Spirit upon all flesh,
and your sons and your daughters shall prophesy,
and your young men shall see visions,
and your old men shall dream dreams.
(Acts 2:17)

The breath of life, the Holy Spirit, in its simplest and most common manifestation, expresses and makes itself felt in prayer. It is a beautiful thought that wherever people are praying in the world, the Holy Spirit is the living breath of prayer. It is an amazing reality to recognize that whenever prayer is offered throughout the world, be it in the past, in the present or in the future, there is also the presence and action of the Holy Spirit. It is the Holy Spirit that breathes prayer into the hearts of all people in the most varied situations and under the most unexpected conditions.

In Luke 11:13 we read: "If you then who are evil know how to give good gifts to your children, how much more will the heavenly Father give the Holy Spirit to those who ask him." The gift of the Holy Spirit is above all the gifts that help us in our weakness. In Romans 8:26, St. Paul enlightens us with: "The Spirit helps us in our weakness for we do not know how to pray as we ought, but that very Spirit intercedes with sighs too deep for words." With these words we come to the realization of how much the Holy Spirit helps and guides us to pray and gives our prayer a divine dimension.

The church was born in the upper room on Pentecost. This event does not belong only to the past, when the Holy Spirit came upon the Apostles, but it is also for today as the Holy Spirit is still present to us. What a gift Jesus, our God, has given us! I kneel before my Father in heaven, giving thanks to his Son Jesus for this wonderful gift of his Spirit, the Spirit which is continuously recreating me.

In the past I thought of the Holy Spirit as being powerful when it came to evangelization, but now realize he is powerful in all things. The Holy Spirit brings us rest and relief in the midst of toil, refreshment in the midst of the heat of day with its anxieties and struggles, and consolation when the human heart grieves and is tempted to despair. What is hard, he softens; what is frozen, he warms; what is dryness of soul, he refreshes anew.

Whenever I hear or read that the Holy Spirit makes all things new, the realization and truth of these words really hit home. In my everyday living, there is nothing I cannot do, because I can do all through him who strengthens me. When I am weak, he is strong. As long as he and I are working together, I can accomplish whatever it is I need to succeed in life. He makes me new. If I want to change anything in my life, he gives me the strength to do it. He is the Advocate, the Helper, the Guide, and Aide that I need – that we all need. Whether it be changing a job, improving myself, or correcting wrongs in a relationship, I know I have choices and if I pray for guidance from the Holy Spirit, I will receive it.

When one begins trusting in the guidance of the Holy Spirit, life becomes such a blessing. We are contented with less and so much more thankful for all the things we do have. We become less negative. We live in the cocoon of the Holy Spirit and nothing can take away the joy and peace that we feel. We are partners, and shall never be separated from the vine which feeds us. We are one with the Holy Spirit and nothing on this Earth or under this Earth can ever separate us from the love and guidance that the Holy Spirit has given us. Through the power of God's Holy Spirit, we will do great and wondrous things, even greater than we could ever imagine.

As Jesus walked along the road to Emmaus, two of his followers did not recognize him, but suddenly – through the power of the Holy Spirit – their eyes were opened and they knew he was alive. We too, must walk alongside him, and through the power of the Holy Spirit, we too will recognize Jesus as he speaks to us. His words will be just as meaningful to us and we will be able to cry out in recognition of him, "Were not our hearts on fire as we heard him speak of such wondrous things?" (Luke 24:13)

Week Twenty-One
Prayerful Reflection

My Children,

I am asking you to help rebuild my church. I will give you wonderful opportunities to assist me. You will be placed in extraordinary circumstances. For some of you, this may mean fame and position; for others, a quiet life of service. I will provide work that will be satisfying and rewarding to you. Those you serve will reap the benefits because your work will bear much fruit.

Pray for guidance and wisdom so you will understand in which way I wish you to serve me. I am the master builder. I not only create, but re-create. You will be my co-workers. Remember – if I do not build the house, then in vain will the workers labor.

Serve me cheerfully and willingly. Many of you have become nervous soldiers under my command. You say you wish to serve me, but I often find you becoming edgy, irritable and discontented. You are caught up in day-to-day battles which interfere with your work and you do not have the faith to see the victory at the end of the battle. You react strongly to other people's troubles and worry needlessly. Place your loved ones in my care.

The Christian life is filled with warfare, but know and understand that peace is a choice you can make if you learn to rely and trust me completely. Choose peace now! I will teach you how to let go without giving up. Put your trust in me. I will teach you how to relax, even through disappointments and disasters. Commit yourself to me and I will grant you a special peace that goes beyond this world's understanding. Be still and feel my presence. I am one with you. I am closer to you than you could ever imagine. Commit your future to me and I will fill your life with good works and blessings.

I know each and every one of my children in a special, personal way. I am thankful that you wish to serve me. Never forget that I came as one who serves; therefore, if you ask me with purity of heart, I will serve you. I am your Father and I love you. Be confident that I will love you always with a love that is limitless and everlasting. You can never lose my love. My love is divine.

I am a gentle taskmaster. Try to comprehend how much I love you and want only what is best for you. Together we will rebuild my church. You will be a beacon and the light within you will draw others to believe that I AM. Whatever services you perform to make me known to those who have not heard or do not believe in my word will not go unrewarded, and ages to come will call you blessed.

Week Twenty-Two
Inspired Thought

Your True Self

This above all; to thine own self be true, and it must follow,
as the night the day, thou canst not then be false to any man.
(Shakespeare)

Do we appear to others not as we really are? We smile when we are sad. We look as if we are in control when we are really losing it. We cover our true identity, our true feelings. We put on a mask. We do not want others to see our weaknesses. We do not admit we need help for we have pride.

But God knows and understands everything about us and in Jeremiah 1:5, he says: "Before I formed you in the womb, I knew you, and before you were born, I consecrated you." God will not forsake us and through prayer and the power of the Holy Spirit, we are enlightened as to who we really are, our true selves. We no longer have to put on a front or a disguise. We realize that when we are weak, he gives us strength to carry the burden. We can be honest and truthful about our feelings because we are wise enough to know that it doesn't matter how we appear to others. We cannot hide anything from God as he sees what is in our hearts. We are to be true to ourselves and then we cannot be false to anyone.

The time will come when, with elation, you will greet your true self. That part of you who could not face up to failure, who pretended that you had it all together, will meet the true person you have become. You will greet each other, smile, embrace, and welcome one another. You will say to one another: let us sit, drink wine and break bread together. You will once again love the stranger whom you had forsaken. You will give your heart back to that part of you which was lost, the part you ignored, the part who knows you by heart, the part who never stopped loving you, your own true self.

Celebrate! The truth has set you free! You have now found your real self, your more splendid self, the self that you were created to be and have now become!

Week Twenty-Two
Prayerful Reflection

My Children,

Just as an earthly friend would advise and instruct you out of love, this is how I now speak to you. I am your devoted friend and want only what is best for you. All that the Father has taught me, I share with you. You did not choose me. I chose you and appointed you to go and bear fruit – fruit that will last.

Yours is the voice I chose to enlighten others about the gift of salvation and I am depending on you not to fail me. Heaven and Earth will rejoice when a soul that has been lost and is now found enters into the portals of heaven. It is not by accident that my words are called the Good News, for you will not succeed in drawing others to me if you are filled with sorrow and apprehension. The souls you are trying to reach will turn away. If you become an example of sincerity, peace, and joy, others will see your Christ-like manner and believe you were chosen by me to spread the message of salvation. Do not let the trials and tribulations of life fill you with despair.

There is much darkness in the world and many of my children are in danger of losing eternal life. Be a light to my lost sheep. Help them find their way out of the darkness. I know this assignment is not an easy task, but I am the vine and you are my branches. There are times when my branches must be pruned. This is painful to you, but I too suffer because we are one and I experience every cut. But I will bind your wounds with mine and make you whole again. When my branches are pruned, there is new growth. Abide in me in times of affliction and you will bring forth much fruit. If you surrender yourself to suffering, it will prepare you to sympathize with all who suffer. Through your compassion and understanding, you will teach many to trust and believe in my word.

Remember that I am never far from you. I will never abandon you. Call on my Holy Spirit to fall afresh on you. My Spirit will melt you, mold you, fill you, use you, heal you and teach you. You will be filled with power from on high. Go forth, using the gifts I have bestowed on you to preach the Good News. You could never comprehend the immense gratitude I have for those who help save souls. Christianity in action is a joy to behold!

Week Twenty-Three
Inspired Thought

Let It Go!

Be kind to one another, tenderhearted, forgiving one another,
as God in Christ has forgiven you.
(Ephesians 4:32)

I recently read an article about President Clinton. He revealed that his stepfather had been an abusive man. He and his mother had suffered greatly. His stepfather had been an alcoholic and would beat him and his mother. He grew up with this terrible burden of shame and fear. He found it very hard to forgive what this man had done to his mother and himself.

Years later when he was President, Clinton visited South Africa. President Nelson Mandela had just been released after 27 years in prison for his political beliefs. President Clinton asked him, "Do you hate those who imprisoned you?" Mandela replied, "Of course I did, for many years. They took the best years of my life. They abused me physically and mentally. I didn't get to see my children grow up. I hated those who had imprisoned me. Then one day I was working in the quarry, hammering the rocks, and I realized that they had already taken everything except my mind and my heart. Those they could not take away without my permission. I decided not to give them away."

President Clinton asked another question, "When you were released from prison, didn't you feel the hatred rise up in you again?" "Yes, for a moment I did," said Mandela. Then I thought to myself, they have had me for 27 years and if I keep on hating them, they will still have me. I wanted to be free and so I let it go." Then Mandela smiled and said, "And so you too, should let it go!"

Week Twenty-Three
Prayerful Reflection

My Children,

You must always have the capacity to forgive. Those who cannot forgive will never have the power to love divinely. There is potential for good in the worst of my children and potential for sin in the best of them, and when you come to understand this, you will be more generous in forgiving others. Remember that the sun rises on the good and the bad, it rains on the just and the unjust. If you love and forgive only those who love and forgive you, what is so praiseworthy about that? You have been forgiven for your many faults, so you in turn, should forgive as well.

I hear you pray for those who have hurt you and mistreated you. Some things can only be cured by prayer. Leave those things to me. Never let the faults of others lead you into sin by becoming angry or unforgiving towards them. When you pray for them, always remember to include yourself in your prayers. It is important that you lift yourself up to me. It is through prayer that you hear my voice.

I will never forsake you. I will guide you in the paths of righteousness and will bless your comings and goings. I will give you strength and courage to face the challenges ahead. I only ask in return that you forgive one another and that you love greatly, because my children need love the most when they deserve it the least. Through the power of love, you will see the impossible become possible. You will penetrate the most stubborn of hearts to turn to me, and this will fill me with great joy and gratitude.

I never forget a forgiving heart, and I will bless you abundantly each time you show compassion and understanding towards the least of my brethren.

Week Twenty-Four
Inspired Thought

Love Thy Neighbor

If you love those who love you, what credit is that to you?
(Luke 6:32)

Imagine the excitement if archaeologists discovered another gospel. Hoping to clear up misinterpretations, theologians would diligently examine the new texts to gain insights into exactly what Jesus meant when he said such profound statements as, "Love your enemy," and "Pray for those who persecute you. Do good to those who hate you." Do you think we could be let off the hook if the next text read: "Love your enemy except when you are at war," or "Pray for those who persecute you and then get even," or "Do good to those who hate you after you defeat them"? Such a gospel has not been found. We Christians are commanded to live with the words and actions of Jesus recorded by the four evangelists.

The real work for peace begins in our hearts and homes. Sometimes it is easier to love an enemy thousands of miles away rather than deal with an obnoxious relative or nasty neighbor. We must always be reminded that we live in a global village, that we are our brothers' and sisters' keeper, and that whatever we do in violence or hatred towards others, we do to Christ. We must first learn to take the log out of our own eye before we attempt to remove the splinter from the eyes of family members and neighbors. To create a world that truly protects and celebrates life, we Christians have to apply the Gospel according to the words Jesus told us – not to interpret them to fit our own ideas and beliefs.

Let us pray that strength and courage be given to all who work for a world of reason and understanding. Let us pray that the good that is in every person's heart be magnified day by day. Let us pray that all will come to see more clearly that what unites us is greater than that which divides us. Let us pray that we may learn to celebrate our differences. Let us pray that each hour may bring us victory, not of nation over nation, but of triumph over our own errors and weaknesses. Let us pray that the true Spirit of mankind --its joy, its beauty, and its hope-- may live among us. Let us pray that the blessings of peace be ours; the peace to build and grow and plan for the future with confidence.

May the Lord of peace instill in us and in all peoples of the world that peace which only he can bestow.

Week Twenty-Four
Prayerful Reflection

My Children,

> Love is not hate.
> Love is not selfishness.
> Love is not greed.
> Love is not anger.
> Love is not immorality.

Love is not revenge.
Love is not jealousy.
Love is not unforgiveness.

Do not allow the evil one to lead you into sin. Unless you love one another unconditionally, you will never reach the perfection I am. Love without asking for payment in return, and you will become a holy vessel.

I have loved you with an everlasting love. I have called you and you are mine. To love one another is the greatest gift you can give to yourself. Love fills up your senses with the presence of who I am. You will come to know and understand my ways in a more intimate fashion.

I am love, and when you love, I reside fully in you. Only when you love one another as I love you, will you receive the peace and joy that surpasses all understanding, - which will never leave you – not even for a moment.

Week Twenty-Five
Inspired Thought

Reflecting on the Writings of <u>Kahil Gibran</u>

Jesus said, "Do not stop him; for whatever is not against you is for you."
(Luke 9:50)

I began to reflect on what Kahil Gibran wrote in his book <u>The Divinity of Man:</u>

"Spring came and nature began speaking in the murmur of the brooks and in the smiles of the flowers; and the soul of man was made happy and content. Then suddenly nature became furious and lay waste the beautiful city, and man forgot his laughter, his sweetness and his kindness. In one hour a frightful, blind force had destroyed what it had taken generations to build. Terrifying death seized man in his claws and crushed him. Ravaging fires consumed man and his goods; a deep and terrifying night hid the beauty of life under a shroud of ashes. The fearful elements raged and destroyed man, his habitations, and all his handiwork. Amidst this frightful thunder of destruction from the bowels of the earth, amidst all this misery and ruin stood a poor soul, gazing upon all this from a distance, and meditating sorrowfully upon the weakness of man and the power of God.

The soul heard the wailing of mothers and of the hungry children, and she shared their suffering. The soul pondered the smallness of man, and she recalled how only yesterday the children of man had slept safely in their homes, but today they were homeless fugitives, bewailing their beautiful city. Gazing upon it from a distance, their hope turned to despair, their joy to sorrow, their life of peace to warfare.

The soul suffered with the broken-hearted who were caught in the iron claws of sorrow, pain and despair. As the soul stood there pondering, she whispered into the ear of silence: 'Behind all this creation, there is eternal wisdom that brings forth wrath and destruction, but which will yet bring forth unpredictable beauty, since fire, thunder, and tempests are to the Earth what hatred, envy and evil are to the human heart.'

While I saw the afflicted nation groaning in pain, memory brought to mind all the calamities and tragedies that have been enacted on the stage of time. I saw man throughout history erecting towers, palaces, temples on the face of the Earth; and I saw the Earth turn her fury upon them and snatch them back into her bosom. I saw strong men building impregnable castles and I observed artists embellishing their walls with paintings; then I saw the Earth open her mouth and swallow all that the skillful hands and the luminous minds of genius had shaped, and I knew that Earth is like a beautiful bride who needs no ornaments to heighten her loveliness, but is content with the green grass of her fields, the golden sands of her seashores, and the precious stones on her mountains. Then I saw man in his divinity standing like a giant in the midst of wrath and destruction, like a pillar of light; man stood amidst the ruins of Babylon, Nineveh, and Pompeii, and as he stood, he sang the song of immortality: "Let the Earth take that which is hers, for I, man, have no ending."

This is an article that could have been written today as we hear of wars and natural disasters, and have experienced the tragedy of 9/11. But it was written by a man called Kahil Gibran around 1920. He was born in Lebanon, but considered himself an Arab. Reading about his life and his origins emphasized once again to me that God works through all people and all nations. We are all God's children and we cannot condemn a whole nation's people because of the inhuman actions of a few fanatics. A few rotten apples do not spoil a whole nation. Imagine the loss to us all had Kahil Gibran's writings never been published because of his race, color or creed. If we allow it, prejudice becomes a cancer that destroys from within.

Week Twenty-Five
Prayerful Reflection

My Children,

I am aware of all that is going on upon the Earth today. Do you think I who formed the eye do not see? I see all. Do you think that I who shaped the ear cannot hear? I hear all. Do you think that I who have created the hearts of my people do not know what they contain? I see the evil in some hearts, but there are many hearts that are filled with love. They surround you. Use your eyes and ears spiritually and you will become aware of them. Cling to those who are good and together you will become an army. Avoid those who are evil, lest they bring you down to hell.

I have commanded you to go forth and teach others what you have learned from me. In some hearts, my words will take hold for a while, but earthly attractions will soon make my words fade. In other hearts, my words will take hold and succeed in bringing me many lost sheep.

Do not become discouraged. Do not grow tired of setting the correct example. This is not an easy task that I ask of you. Alone it is impossible, but for you, with me working through you, nothing is impossible. Your strength will come from spending time with me in prayer. Through prayer you will receive the knowledge, discernment and understanding of how to address my people. Through prayer my will for you will be made clear. Through prayerful union with me, your lives will be changed. You will be enlightened to realize how much I love you and you will have begun your journey to sainthood.

Week Twenty-Six
Inspired Thought

Jesus, the Son

And a voice came from heaven,
"You are my Son, the beloved; with you I am well pleased."
(Mark 1:11)

Did Jesus ever concern himself with the fact that he could never come up to the expectations of his Father? Many sons of famous fathers feel inferior. They believe that they will never reach the heights their fathers did.

Did Jesus feel like that? I don't believe so. There is no rivalry, no jealousy, and no competitiveness in his relationship with his Father as there are in so many father/son relationships. Jesus always gives the glory and praise to his Father. Why is Jesus so generous in praising his Father? It is because his Father is worthy of praise. The love that God has for all humanity, for his creation, is proven when he sent himself, as his Son, to redeem the human race. Jesus is one with the Father. He is assured of the Father's love for him. He is obedient to the will of his Father. He loves the Father and wants to please him. Jesus' love for the Father binds them as one, and this love is so powerful that it even conquers death. In John 11: 41, before raising Lazarus from the dead, Jesus looked upward to heaven and prayed: "Father, I thank you for having heard me. I know that you always hear me. I have said this for the sake of the crowd standing here, so that they may believe that you sent me." Jesus never hesitated in giving all the praise and glory to his Father.

Pray that all fathers be worthy of the praise of their sons. Pray that all sons be obedient to their loving fathers just as Jesus was to his Father. What a wonderful world it would be!

Week Twenty-Six
Prayerful Reflection

My Children,

When you lift your arms and voices in praise and thanksgiving, calling on the mystery of the Holy Trinity, three beings in one God, you are opening yourselves to receiving a powerful change in your lives. I am your Father, Jesus is your brother and the Holy Spirit is the loving link that connects us all to become one. When you give praise through the Holy Trinity it gives me much pleasure, and in return you are blessed three-fold! When you do so, you are bestowing on me the ultimate praise, and the light that is within you is giving witness to others of my glory. Through you, the heavens are declaring my glory and the firmament proclaiming my handiwork.

A city does not need the sun or the moon to shine on it, for it is my glory that gives it light. My Son is the light of the world. He is the radiance of my glory. My son came to Earth so that you could fully understand my glory. My word became flesh and dwelled among you so that you could see his glory, a glory full grace and truth. My Son honored me by fulfilling my purpose for him on Earth, which was to take upon himself the sins of the world, thereby redeeming the human race, in order that mankind could once again achieve the glory of heaven.

You are not here by accident. I have a purpose for each of you. You are commanded to go forth and spread the mystery of the Trinity and the power of the cross. I have given you the privilege of enlightening others to the gift of salvation which comes through my Son, Jesus Christ. I have given you the Holy Spirit which will develop in you a Christ-like character, inspiring you to bring those who are lost to me. You are to aid me in revealing my saving grace to them so that they too will learn and reap the benefits of my Son's saving grace.

Always remember to dwell on the mystery of the Holy Trinity, three Gods in one, and in return you will always be showered with many blessings from on high.

Week Twenty-Seven
Inspired Thought

The Flight into Egypt

Out of Egypt, I have called My Son!
(Matthew 2:15)

What does the flight into Egypt, something that happened twenty centuries ago, mean to men and women who have never crossed a desert, never ridden a donkey, and never clasped a child who was in danger? Mary, our Blessed Mother, embracing Jesus in her loving and protective arms flees into Egypt. The hands of Mary hold Jesus in love and fear on the trip through the desert. Life has its ups and downs, even for Mary.

She remembers how the words of the angel announcing to her that she was to bear a child were hard for her to comprehend. The visit to Elizabeth was sheer joy when she heard the 'Hail Mary' proclaimed. Under Mary's own Immaculate Heart, the Sacred Heart of Jesus was beating, mingled with her own blood and timed to the tempo of her own pulse. Small wonder the words of the Magnificat poured forth!

She remembers how she was thrust into anguish because her husband Joseph had filled her with questions about her pregnancy. It is an angel who soothes and comforts Joseph's spirit and lifts Mary's heart with the words, "Do not be afraid!" She remembers the doors of Bethlehem's inns being slammed shut in their faces. "He came unto his own and his own received him not."

At the birth of Jesus, she remembers the Gloria being sung by the angels, the visit of the shepherds, and the Magi bearing gifts. The Magi had hardly departed when Joseph shakes Mary out of her slumber and tells her that the child is in danger and they must flee to Egypt. We see the hands of Mary hugging her child as a sea of sand stretches before them and Herod's soldiers threaten them from afar.

They learn that life not only has its ups and downs, but that God always does the unexpected. Here are the three people closest to God on Earth and how are they rewarded? Frightened, they must flee into Egypt. Let us contemplate this picture and realize that this is God who is in flight! It is God's Mother and the man nearest to Christ who are in fright and flight!

Let us remember the times we are frightened and feel a need to fly to safety. Let us remember Mary, Joseph and Jesus in their flight and how God provided a safe haven for them. He will do the same for us if we remember that fear is useless, what is needed is trust!

Week Twenty-Seven
Prayerful Reflection

My Children,

You are fearful about many things that according to my ways have no importance. You have not yet learned to trust me fully.

You are afraid and filled with fear. When you truly come to know me you will realize that all your worry and fears are of no value. Worry and fear have never been known to change any problem or situation. Fear is useless. Fear is only a feeling. It is the same as saying, "I feel hungry," or "I feel tired," or "I feel lonely." These feelings can not harm you. Only when you give into your fears can they cause you to falter. Do not dwell on thoughts that are negative. They come from the evil one. Learn to believe that through me, you will be able to conquer all of your fears.

Many of you fear death. There is no death. I have given you the gift of eternal life. Living in sin is the only death. Avoid sin at all costs; otherwise, you will have condemned yourselves. Never grow weary of doing what is right and just. Sin violates my commandments. It is sin that separates you from me. Resolve your disagreements with one another. Get your affairs in order. Forgive as I have forgiven you. Rid all hatred from your heart. Settle your accounts before it is too late.

I am a merciful God. Repent. Give me your contrite hearts. If you must fear anything, fear the loss of paradise. Time is fleeting. Do not lose the gift of everlasting life and the fullness of life I have given you from the cross.

I suffered willingly to take upon myself the sins of the world because of my passionate love for each and every one of you. You must hunger and thirst for eternal life with the same passion. Only then will you start to live your lives according to my holy will. Come! See what I have prepared for you!

Week Twenty-Eight
Inspired Thought

Peace that is not of this World

For Christ himself is our way of peace.
He has made peace between us by making us one family,
breaking down the wall of contempt that used to separate us.
(Ephesians 2:14)

Jesus did not promise us peace in this world. In John 14:27 he said: "Peace is my farewell to you, my peace is my gift to you; I do not give it to you as the world gives peace. Do not be distressed or fearful." Perhaps we will never have peace in this life. We must pray and work towards peace, but perhaps it will never happen, because there are too many people who do not love. Jesus himself said that brother would fight against brother, and mother against daughter.

Peace is not the absence of problems. The peace that comes only from God remains with us regardless of life's circumstances. Peace comes in knowing that our Father is continually with us. Even though we cannot see the air we breathe, we know it is always there, and although we cannot see God, he is always with us. He alone can give us the peace that surpasses all understanding.

Paul prayed for the thorn in his flesh to be removed. When this didn't happen, we read in 2 Corinthians 12:9 how Paul reconciled himself to the Lord's words: "My grace is sufficient for you, for in weakness, power reaches perfection." Like Paul, despite our hardships, God's grace will be sufficient to get us through. He will supply all our needs in ways that are ultimately best for us. We will have tribulation in the world, but if we abide in Christ, there will be inner peace, even in tribulation. If we walk in the peace of God, we will not panic or be filled with anxiety. The Holy Spirit is called the Comforter for a reason: we must learn to let go and let God. Paul teaches us that through acceptance we gain peace.

How do we try to get this peace? Mary, sister of Martha, is our model. We are so much like Martha. She was restless. Our pace also becomes hectic when we try to serve others. It is hard for us to slow down. We put ourselves on a schedule and nothing will deter us from it. Jesus was not putting Martha down because she was serving, but because she was not taking the time to be present to the moment. Mary's mission was also to serve, but she set her priorities straight. Mary's manner clearly revealed a soul at rest. She had the imperishable quality of a gentle and quiet spirit which is precious in the eyes of God. Mary had chosen the better portion and it would not be taken from her. When we get caught up in trivial matters of unimportance, let us hear Jesus speak to our hearts: "Come! Sit with me. Let us spend some quiet time together. Let us not waste a moment of this precious time!"

Week Twenty-Eight
Prayerful Reflection

My Children,

We are standing on holy ground. Whenever two or more of you gather, I am in your midst. Every Wednesday as you come through the door, I am filled with happiness to see you. I am present at every one of your meetings. I hear you speak. I hear you share your experiences. My heart overflows with gratitude at the sound of your voices lifted in praise to me. You are acknowledging my presence!

My cup overflows with love and appreciation for all of you so dedicated in attending our weekly meetings. I see in your hearts how you enjoy coming to this place of worship, and I also look forward to these meetings with great anticipation. It gives me great pleasure to see your spiritual growth from week to week.

Many of my children have forgotten me, and it comforts me to hear you give witness so that others may believe that I AM. You must welcome all who enter. You are a powerful vehicle to save those who are in darkness. Send no one away without a word of cheer. Impress on their hearts that you care. Do not feel that you have to solve everyone's problems. Just show them love. I am love. I will place in their hearts the knowledge that your love is filling them up with me, the Lord of all. Love breaks down all difficulties. Love builds up successes. Love is the destroyer of all evil. My world is broken because my children do not love. When you love, you will feel my presence in your life and it is love which brings harmony, beauty, joy and peace. Love my people and then let me do my work. My broken world needs you. I need you to plant the seed and to water it, but you must leave the growth to me. I am with you always. Live completely in my presence. I look forward to our next meeting! I will continue to bless you all abundantly!

Week Twenty-Nine
Inspired Thought

Lest We Forget

If anyone says, "I love God," but keeps hating his brother, he is a liar;
for if he does not love his brother, whom he has seen,
how can he love God whom he has never seen?
(1 John 4:20)

On PBS, there was a biography of Elie Weisel, Jewish historian and author. He started to explain how important our memory is. If we do not remember certain important events, they will be forgotten. In many instances, that would be a tragedy as we can only learn to correct injustices by remembering how and why they occurred. The only way we keep events and people alive is by remembering them. Weisel searched his mind to remember events that happened to him and his parents when they were in a concentration camp during World War II.

Steven Spielberg, director of many movies, made a documentary of personal experiences of the holocaust so that these horrendous occurrences would not be forgotten. He asked many of the survivors to record their stories before they died. Elie Weisel was one of the survivors asked to contribute events from his memory.

Spielberg has also made other films about the events of World War II. In one instance he interviewed military personnel, servicemen and women, and anyone who had any input as to what happened in this war. He has also made movies about slavery, racism, and other historical events. His movies have enlightened us all to the plights of the past.

The Wind Talkers is a film that depicts the true story of the Navajo Indian Tribe whose role in World War II was kept secret until recently. During this war, the enemy was able to decipher many of our codes. This was detrimental to the survival of our troops. The idea of using Navajo Indians to transmit messages in their native language was developed to deter this. This turned out to be very successful since theirs is a language that is passed orally from one generation to another, and cannot be found in books. There was no way the enemy could decipher these messages. These Navajo Indians helped win the war, but since the success of this mission relied on the secrecy of this code, it was kept in strictest confidence. After the war ended, what the Navajo Indians had accomplished was still not disclosed. The reasoning behind this was that the Navajo code could be useful in case of another war. Finally, almost 50 years later, as a result of the release of this film, we have now recognized these Navajo Indians as heroes. It would have been shameful if this historical event would have been forgotten and these men not received the honor due them. Hopefully, by watching films such as these, we will come to understand that intolerance is ugly, that we must learn from mistakes of the past, and that we must be watchful to see these injustices do not occur in the future.

Alex Haley wrote the book Roots. On a trip to Africa, he uncovered the roots of his ancestors before his heritage would have been forgotten. The book was made into a film, which was a huge television success.

It showed how hatred of people based on race or culture is wrong. Alex Haley remembered his ancestors and what they went through, and we benefited from his remembering. What a lesson it taught us about bigotry!

Many of us do not know about our past because we did not take the time to write it down, or we never asked questions, or maybe we just weren't interested. Years later, when it is too late, our curiosity piques, and we sometimes regret not learning more about where we came from.

It was something Elie Weisel said that started me thinking about all this. In the Old Testament, it is written: "If you are my witnesses, then I am God. If you are not my witnesses, then I do not exist."

We have been given the power of the Holy Spirit in order to witness to the gift of salvation. The story of salvation continues because people talk about it, write about it, sing about it, and celebrate holidays associated with it. It is so important for us to remember that what we have received as a gift, we must give as a gift. If no one spoke about the gift of salvation for hundreds of years and the Bible was not read but forgotten, God would not exist for those who are to come after us. They would be like the unenlightened, in the farthest corners of the Earth, who never heard of God, Christ, and His Holy Spirit.

Paul tells us in Romans 10:14: "How can they call on him in whom they have not believed? And how are they to believe in him if they have not heard? How are they to proclaim him if they have not been sent? How beautiful are the feet of those who bring Good News."

Week Twenty-Nine
Prayerful Reflection

My Children,

Do you wish to know what love is? Love is seeing the good in all my people. This is how I love. I see the good in all of you. If I have created it, and it is of me, it is good. Are you surrounded by those whom you find difficult to love – those who seem intolerable, annoying, immoral – those who are negative – who burden you and weigh you down? Look for the good in them and you will fall in love.

Each of you is my disciple. I have called each one of you by name. I have probed you and I know you. You are wonderfully and fearfully made. I know all your actions and nothing is hidden from me. I look for the good in you and love you unconditionally. Follow my example and look for the good in all.

You will encounter those who do evil, who seek to destroy my kingdom. If they present themselves to you, you are required to tell them the Good News. If they accept, a blessing upon you! If not, leave them to me. Do not become discouraged. They are also my children and I love them. Seek the best in others and you will find it. My words, "Love others as I have loved you," will take on a truth never realized before. And those who you believed to be unlovable according to human standards, you will love in a divine manner that you never thought possible. The way to victory in any situation, no matter how hopeless it may appear, is through love. I am love. When you love, I am present, and through my Holy Spirit, the power to change all things to the good will happen. I am not only the Creator; I am the Re-Creator of all that is good.

You are my good and faithful servants. I send you forth to teach others to seek the good in all of humankind. Many healings will take place. The lion will lie down with the lamb and peace will be restored to all nations as hearts of stone are changed into hearts of love.

Week Thirty
Inspired Thought

Called to the Catholic Faith

We believe in one holy, catholic, and apostolic church.
We acknowledge one baptism for the forgiveness of sins.
We look for the resurrection of the dead and the life of the world to come.
Amen!
(Nicene Creed)

Lord, you have given us the whole loaf. Why do some of us only take half? You lead us with your rod and your staff though we may be of many different faiths. There are many paths to you and all of them are hallowed, but being a Catholic, I believe I am partaking of the whole loaf. Taste and see the goodness of the Lord! You have given us so many gifts to help sustain us in our Catholic faith:

The Church (His Body) – which it is said in the scriptures "not even the gates of hell shall destroy." (Matthew 16:18) It includes the community of saints who have gone on before us, and those of us on Earth who are striving to be worthy of spending eternity in his kingdom.

<u>The Mass</u> – It is a remembrance of the passion of Christ and his gift of living bread which strengthens us to become more like him.

<u>The Holy Eucharist</u> – The body and blood of Jesus, in which our Lord manifests his physical presence here on Earth, and our heavenly sustenance.

<u>Our Blessed Mother Mary</u> – A role model for us all; she is without sin and was chosen by the Father to be the mother of our blessed Lord and Savior, Jesus Christ.

<u>The Blessed Angels</u> – Messengers of God, who watch over us, guide, and protect us.

<u>The Bible</u> – Inspired by those who were called to write it many years ago, it still inspires us to holiness today; the living word of God.

<u>The Sacraments</u> – which are Baptism, Confirmation, Holy Eucharist, Marriage, Holy Orders, Reconciliation, and the Anointing of the Sick. Through each of the sacraments we are strengthened and become personally more connected with our Lord.

<u>The Pope</u> – He is our vicar here on earth; a spiritual guide to keep us on the right path.

<u>The Cardinals, Bishops, Priests, Brothers, Sisters, Missionaries and all other Religious.</u> – They are all those who help us to understand your word and along with ourselves, aspire to holiness, despite our humanness.

<u>Lay People</u> – Men and women who unselfishly dedicate their lives to serving the Lord and spreading the word.

Lord, thank you for the many tools that you avail to us in our community of the Catholic Church. Teach us to use them to bring us closer to you and to build upon and strengthen the foundation of our faith and to spread your Good News to all. Thank you for instilling in us your Spirit, who is our Counselor, Advocate, and Truth. It is through your Holy Spirit that we receive the fruits which help us to become more like Jesus. It is the Holy Spirit who teaches and helps us to pray. It is the Holy Spirit that opens our minds to the mysteries of God. It is the Holy Spirit that the Father sends to us who will instruct and guide us. It is the Holy Spirit, who not only calls us to the Catholic Faith, but inspires us to call others to the Catholic Faith so that they can partake of your goodness as well.

Week Thirty
Prayerful Reflection

My Children,

You are the rock upon which I build my church. My church is not one made of bricks and mortar, but of human flesh and faith. Yet you know that being faithful or holy will not make you immune from disaster or wicked events. Sometimes I calm the storm that my children are in; and other times I calm my children amid the storm. Events can occur in your lives which produce such consuming anxiety and overwhelming fear that your focus becomes on the disaster alone. Do you realize that when earthquakes, floods, epidemics, and threats of terrorism invade your environment, you no longer concern yourself with insignificant issues? It is during these times that you learn to understand what is truly important in life. It is during these times that I want you to realize that my church will sustain you through both good times and bad. How many of you return to my church for reassurance in troubled times, only to abandon it again when the storm has passed?

I have provided my church for your protection. The evil one trembles when he sees the weakest of my saints kneeling in prayer. Use my church to break the chain of sin that surrounds my people by submerging yourself in deep prayer. In days of trouble, trust that I will protect and comfort you, as you journey through this quickly fading life. I am your light and your salvation. With me at your side, whom should you fear? Even though your enemies attack and wage war against you, I am your refuge. My church is your refuge. Why be afraid? When disaster strikes, pray for guidance and strength to do what is right in my sight.

When all is well, I come to you in a whisper, but when you experience pain and disaster, I shout to get your attention. It is in times of trouble and turmoil that you most clearly hear my voice, and come to realize that my church is a refuge to comfort and calm you. The next time you are faced with an insurmountable problem, remember that I and my church are shouting to get your attention.

Always focus on what is truly valuable in your life; the love of your family and friends, the comfort of your home and neighborhood, and most importantly, never lose your desire to dwell in the loveliness of my heavenly house for all eternity. But for now, I implore you to dwell in the loveliness of my earthly house, my church, not only through the storm, but through the calm as well.

Week Thirty-One
Inspired Thought

All Things to All People

See how they lie in wait for me!
Fierce men conspire against me for no offense or sin of mine.
O Lord, I have done no wrong, yet they attack me.
Arise to defend me; look at my plight!
(Psalm 59:1-5)

Many years ago there was an actor named Lon Chaney. Lon Chaney had the ability, with the help of make-up, to play many character parts. Because of this, he became known as "The Man of a Thousand Faces." This title could readily apply to Jesus Christ. Jesus has the ability to appear to people in many different ways. He is all things to all men; he is the Man of Sorrows, the Shepherd, the King of Kings, etc.

To me, Jesus appears most dramatically as a lawyer. When one breaks the law, a good lawyer is needed. An honorable lawyer defends his client. He is filled with knowledge and wisdom. A moral attorney not only practices according to the letter of the law, but also according to the spirit of the law. He is expected to be trustworthy and protects the confidence of his client. Whether the accused is innocent or guilty makes no difference to the lawyer's defense of his client. He must still defend his client to the best of his ability. If proven guilty, he will try to get the accused off with the lightest sentence.

Let us imagine Jesus as a lawyer. Seated at the bench in the high court is God, the judge. The jury box is filled with people representing all walks of life who will weigh the evidence. The prosecuting attorney is Satan. Jesus is the defending attorney. The human race is on trial to have the consequences of a previous verdict overturned. Men, women, and children are pleading for mercy and reconciliation with the Father, and to have the gates of heaven re-opened and eternal life restored.

The judge asks Jesus to call his witnesses. Adam takes the stand followed by Eve. God, the judge, asks Satan to call his first witness. The serpent slithers forth. More witnesses are called. Then the jury leaves to deliberate and comes back with a verdict of guilty and a recommendation for mercy. The judge agrees, but there is a huge penalty. The law has been broken and someone must pay the debt. Jesus steps forth and volunteers to pay the debt. The judge and jury are satisfied. A date is set.

The execution of Jesus takes place on Good Friday at a place called Calvary. The debt has been paid in full. After the sentence is carried out, Paradise is restored. Merciful Jesus! Thank you!

Week Thirty-One
Prayerful Reflection

My Children,

Tonight is a special night! It is like no other night in your life. It is a night of remembrance.

Each of you will receive special gifts I have prepared just for you. You may think you are unworthy to receive the gifts of my Holy Spirit, but the more you desire my gifts, the more generous I will be. Do you think that I, who willingly gave up my life for you, would withhold my gifts from you? I am showering you with the gifts of wisdom, knowledge, faith, healing, miracles, prophecy, discernment and tongues. Pray to my Holy Spirit for guidance and your gifts will bear much fruit.

When Saint Bernadette was asked, "What work can you do to serve the Lord? You are so weak and ill." She answered, "My illness is my work. He has called me to serve him through my illness."

Anything you do for me is never too small or too unworthy. The works that you perform, no matter how insignificant you might think they are, are precious in my sight.

Week Thirty-Two
Inspired Thought

God, Did I Hear You Laugh at Me Today?

*It is the heart that is not yet sure of its God that
is afraid to laugh in his presence.
(George Macdonald – 1879)*

God, you who are so overburdened with problems and concerns of the world, did I hear you laugh at me today? I'm sure if there is anyone that can make you laugh, it's me.

Did you laugh when I ranted and raved like a crazy woman after I spilled that bottle of wine on my new carpet? How about when I parked my car in a no-parking zone, only to return and find a $75.00 ticket? I had a convulsion which almost turned into a stroke. I bet that gave you a good laugh!

Remember the night I had twenty five people coming for dinner and nothing turned out right, and there I was, crying in the kitchen thinking the world had come to an end; did you think I was funny then? Did you laugh the morning I ran three blocks to get the bus, only to have it pull away just as I reached it? I sat on the curb gasping for air, thinking I wasn't going to make it.

Lord, in your infinite wisdom, you must look at us mortals who have such a tendency to make mountains out of molehills and wonder why these humans frustrate themselves with such minor occurrences. You are absolutely right in laughing at our stupidity. Give us the wisdom to understand that we must not get upset over minor, incidental annoyances that are bound to occur in our everyday lives. Help us to understand that if we learn to laugh at ourselves, we will be the better for it.

Lord, I would like to ask you a question. I'm curious about your laugh. Does it begin with a small grin, like a bit of sunshine peaking through a cloud? Does it then burst into a full warm summer glow? Or do you store it up and then let it come out like thunder, full and boisterous?

God, I'd like to tell you something. If you can laugh at me, I guess I can learn to laugh at myself. By the way God, I'm glad I made you laugh today because if anyone deserves a good laugh, it's you!

Week Thirty-Two
Prayerful Reflection

My Children,

Do you realize how precious the gift of life is that I have given you? If you did, you would not waste time. Most of your days are spent worrying about situations that will never happen. Instead of enjoying life, you have burdened yourself with cares that most times should not concern you. You worry about your family, health, money and relationships. I have blessed you with many gifts, but instead of allowing them to give you pleasure, you are apprehensive. When problems arise, try to resolve them, but if all fails, trust the words of scripture, "With God, all things are possible." Learn to let go and put everything completely and totally under my control.

I wish you to have the fullness of life and there is only one way this is possible. Look at the positive and ignore the negative events that occur in your life. Look around and start to enjoy your environment, your neighborhood, your home and your garden. I have given you so many gifts to enjoy. Learn to use and enjoy your possessions; share them generously with others. You will not take them with you when you leave this Earth.

Appreciate your family and friends. No one is perfect and people may have many faults, but leave them to me. Learn to see the good in them if they appear to be different from you and make a habit of praying for them. I will hear your prayer. I am a just and merciful God. I have compassion for all my children.

A sick person needs a physician, but many times you worry about your health needlessly. This interferes with your peace of mind and plays havoc with your health. Relax into your prayer time with me and you will be renewed. You will become a new creation mentally, physically and spiritually. Time on this earth passes very quickly. Before it is too late, take pleasure in life's little things.

Be willing to get rid of the life you have planned so as to enter the life that is waiting for you. Awaken to greet the new day with joy and enthusiasm for the adventures that lie ahead. I am with you every step of the way. I am your courage when you face fear; I am your peace when you are anxious; I am your solace when you are sad, and I am the love that surrounds you. Feel that love! It is an armor of protection which no evil or hate can penetrate to disturb you.

Life is a banquet, but most of my children are starving because they are not enjoying the precious gift of life I have given them. This is the day I have created. Rejoice and be glad in it! Be at peace and do not be afraid! Remember, when my angels came to announce the birth of my Son, they first sang about peace. Shalom!

Week Thirty-Three
Inspired Thought

Who Told You That You Were Naked?

So have no fear of them; for nothing is covered up that will not be
uncovered, and nothing is secret that will not become known.
What I say in the dark, tell in the light,
and what you hear whispered proclaim from the housetops.
(Matthew 10:26-28)

"Who told you that you were naked?" These are the words spoken to Adam and Eve in the garden after they had disobeyed God's orders not to eat from the tree of knowledge. This scripture was read at the feast of the Immaculate Conception and the words hit me like a thunderbolt. I have experienced this so many times: the way in which the Holy Spirit speaks through scripture, helping me to interpret God's word.

Adam and Eve had never noticed their nakedness before. It seemed natural to them. They were comfortable with it. Only after they sinned did they become aware they were unclothed. They wanted to cover themselves. They wanted to hide. They felt that if they were clothed, their sinful deed would be hidden. It would make them feel safe, as though God could not see their sins if their bodies were covered.

How often have we felt that way? How often have we found that when we have done wrong, our first impulse is to hide, to cover our misdeeds? When we do something that is not pleasing to God, we may feel that all eyes are on us, that everyone knows. We are ashamed. When we give in to temptation, we start to feel guilty, uncomfortable, and uneasy. We too, may want to hide; to cover ourselves; to have someone close the lights; for if we are in the dark, no one will see the wrong we have done. Yet no one else might really be aware of what we have done; only God knows.

We can try to identify with the way Adam was feeling when God asked him, "Who told you that you were naked? Have you eaten from the tree I warned you about?" (Genesis 3:11-12) We try to deny it or blame someone else. Adam blamed Eve. Adam had the freedom of choice, as we all do when it comes to yielding to temptation. How different things might have been if one or both of them were strong enough not to succumb to temptation.

No human is perfect and God is aware of this fact. We have all sinned. The spirit is so willing, but the flesh is so weak. We pray for strength to not give in to temptation. We pray not to offend God. We truly do not want to hurt God for he deserves only love and goodness from us. We are grateful for God's mercy and forgiveness.

When we are about to do something offensive to God, perhaps remembering the words God spoke to Adam, "Who told you that you were naked?" might help us to stop before we commit the misdeed.

Mary Moussot

Week Thirty-Three
Prayerful Reflection

My Children,

I have chosen to reach past the sun, the moon, and the stars in order to take your hand, but you do not see me. Most of my children do not even believe in my existence. Have I come all this way for naught? For us to have a relationship, we must spend time together. Is there a better way to spend your time? I have all the answers that you are searching for. Sit with me. Talk with me. Listen to me. I know you intimately, but you do not know me. Your life will change when you truly become one with me. I will lead you on the right path.

Week Thirty-Four
Inspired Thought

Body of Christ

But rejoice insofar as you are sharing Christ's sufferings, so that you may also be glad and shout for joy when his glory is revealed.
(1 Peter 4:16)

In Colossians 1:24, Saint Paul tells us: "We make up in our bodies what is lacking in the suffering of Christ." It makes me think about what could possibly be lacking in the suffering of Christ.

When God decided to enter our world in the person of Jesus, he accepted the limitations of finite human existence. In his short time on Earth, there was only so much Jesus could experience as a human being, so he chose the cross as a vehicle of grace through which to glorify the Father. Jesus revealed that the Father could be present even in the midst of unspeakable suffering and a torturous death. If the Father could be present there on the cross, then he can be with us in all circumstances.

Still, there was only so much Jesus could suffer in his short life on Earth. Jesus never had to bury his mother, endure the loss of a spouse, or weep at the death of his own child. Jesus never had to deal with terminal illness or bear the cross of old age. Perhaps his followers are to make up what is missing in the suffering of Christ. We are truly honored that God our Father, thinks so highly of us that through our sufferings we can participate with Jesus, his Son, in this mystery of redemption.

By participating with Jesus in the redemption of humanity, we have formed the Body of Christ. Because of our faith in God and our hope in our own resurrection, we shine the light of grace into the darkest and saddest recesses of our individual lives.

During the season of Lent, we fast, make sacrifices, and pray the Stations of the Cross. We do all these things not only to be present with Jesus on his way to his death on Calvary, but also to realize that he is present with us as we journey towards our Calvary. Lent reminds us to unite our suffering to Christ's, and Christ's to that of our brothers and sisters in the world.

In Galatians 6:14, Paul makes this clear by telling us: "May I never boast of anything except the cross of our Lord Jesus Christ, by which the world has been crucified to me and I to the world. From now on, let no one make trouble for me; for I carry the marks of Jesus branded on my body." When we begin to believe and live these words, we will truly belong to the Body of Christ.

Week Thirty-Four
Prayerful Reflection

My Children,

When you find that life is just unbearable, when you are surrounded by illness, affliction and insurmountable problems, hold no bitterness towards me. I am not responsible for life's tragedies.

I am the Creator of all that is good and I desire the human race to be filled with the joy and fullness of life. I am a positive God who believes that good will always triumph over evil. All that is negative comes from the evil one. Never forget this. I love you and want only what is best for you.

If you go through the valley of the shadow of death, if you must say goodbye to those whom you have loved, if you are suffering, if you are unjustly persecuted, take heart; take courage. I am more than adequate to wipe all tears from your eyes and ease all your pain and suffering. I am your companion and comforter on your journey of life. Live in the present. Do not dwell on yesterday or be anxious about tomorrow. In every circumstance that you encounter, make me a part of your life. No matter where you go or whom you are with, you must live completely in my presence. Only then will you have the courage and strength to face the obstacles that occur in your life.

Your prayers are very powerful. You must not only pray for others, but also pray for yourself. I want all of my people to be of one heart and one mind. No one can ever separate you from my love unless you permit it. My love is for all!

Week Thirty-Five
Inspired Thought

Forgive One Another

For if you forgive others their trespasses,
your heavenly Father will also forgive you;
but if you do not forgive others,
neither will your Father forgive your trespasses.
(Matthew 6:14-16)

Last Saturday night at Mass, our pastor gave a wonderful sermon on forgiveness. He spoke of the movie "Dead Man Walking," which is a true story based on a book by Sr. Helen Prejean about a criminal's life. Susan Sarandon portrayed Sr. Helen, and Sean Penn portrayed a hardened criminal, who had committed many evil deeds. The nun becomes interested in this particular man and visits him frequently. In the beginning, he is very sarcastic and cruel to her, but through her kindness and patience, she is able to spiritually turn him around. He is in darkness, but because of her loving aid, she brings him into the light. She tries to change his death sentence to life imprisonment but fails, and the movie ends with the man going to the electric chair for all of the evil deeds he committed. Nevertheless, all is not lost because she was successful in leading him to repent and desire forgiveness.

One of his victims was a woman whom he maliciously raped. Even though justice is served and he is put to death for all the crimes he committed, this woman still cannot bring herself to forgive him. Her life had become a living hell of hatred.

After Sr. Helen contacts her and as they talk, the woman reveals her grief and anger. Sr. Helen is able to convey to her that no matter how terrible the sin, God has told us to forgive "70 times 7." Even when it is most difficult to do, we must first forgive if we ourselves wish to be forgiven. The victim eventually comes to forgive this man for all the horrible acts he committed toward her. She finally puts the memory of his cruelty to rest and goes on with her life. Her hatred against the criminal has vanished and she is at peace, something which she never thought she would ever experience again. This was all due to the intervention of Sister Helen.

The pastor then said the following words, which really had an impact on me. "It was through justice of the law that this convicted criminal was brought to his death. Yet peace and healing did not come to this woman when justice was served; but only by forgiving the man for what he had done to her. Once she truly forgave him, she became a whole person."

Sr. Helen was able to aid the criminal by helping him see the error of his ways. It was likely that in his lifetime not one person had taken the time to be a witness of the love God had for him. Sr. Helen led him out of the darkness of evil into God's holy light. Before he died, he truly understood the meaning of love. Because Sister Helen took the time and effort to show a criminal the way to salvation, she was instrumental in saving a lost soul. And because Sister Helen took the time and effort to teach the way of forgiveness, the victim was able to put aside all hatred and rancor and become a whole person again.

We are called to ponder in our hearts all that will draw us closer to our Lord, and one of the most important prayers is to ask God to show us the way to forgive those who have trespassed against us. Let us gaze upon the picture of the merciful Jesus to remind us how much he has forgiven us our transgressions, and then let us reflect how important it is for us to forgive others who have hurt us. Let us ask ourselves, "Is there anyone that I must forgive?"

Week Thirty-Five
Prayerful Reflection

My Children,

Forgive them for they know not what they do! Heed these words spoken to you from the cross. Wars occur in the world today by those who seek revenge for past offenses against their ancestors. They cannot forgive and forget.

Because of this hatred, the innocent are being punished and suffer greatly. I, your God, am in anguish because these innocent victims cry out to me. There will be much sobbing and lamentation among all the nations if this slaughtering continues. Only love and forgiveness will prevent the destruction of mankind. I am a loving and compassionate God, but I also am a just God. Pity those who have harmed one of my innocent children. Better if they had not been born.

Healing and peace start with forgiving one another. Forgive those who have trespassed against you and the madness will stop. To those who have abandoned you and been disloyal to you – forgive. To those who betrayed you and hurt you deeply – forgive. To those who have abused you and mistreated you – forgive. Erase all past grievances. Delete all hurtful memories. Anger, revenge and bitterness on your part will harm only you, no one else. You may be the innocent victim, but your hatred will destroy you. It will be your downfall as well as the downfall of many others. Learn to look at others through my eyes. Try to understand why they do the things they do. Have a compassionate and understanding heart.

Any injustice done to you is painful. It is a cross you carry, a crown of thorns you wear, and a sword piercing your heart, but I am commanding you to love and to forgive. Melt your hearts of stone and unburden yourselves from the chains you have forged because you have not forgiven. Heed my words to forgive, and you will experience true freedom for the first time in your life. Your spirit will soar and you will be filled with a joy that is not of this world but which comes only from me.

Come! Why do you hesitate? Will you not trust me in this instance that I know what is best for you? Do you not understand all I have done out of love for you? If I can forgive you, why can you not do the same and forgive others?

Week Thirty-Six
Inspired Thought

From a Distance

Behold! I make all things new!
(Revelations 21:5)

(Inspired by my sister, Josephine, whose birthday is celebrated
on the same day as Our Blessed Mother, September 8th)

It was a beautiful church. It had just been restored. Many parishioners visited it every day and were proud that it was in their neighborhood. No matter what time of day, people could enter to pray or just sit quietly. If you sat in the back of the church, you could observe those who arrived and those who left.

Although the altar was clearly visible, at first one did not notice the statue. It was in the corner as if someone was trying to hide it. It was old, it was chipped, and it definitely did not, as someone had once proclaimed, go with the décor of the church's restoration. But for those who knew the statue was there, it was loved. It was a statue of Our Lady, the Blessed Mother. People would kneel before it and from a distance you could sit quietly and watch the transformation that took place in the faces of the men, women, and children as they looked at it. It was wonderful to behold! Some would pray, some would cry, and some would be filled with joy and thanksgiving. Some would talk to the statue as if Mary were truly present. Maybe she was! Over and over again, this scene would take place. Mary was everyone's mother and all had recourse to her. They could tell her their problems without shame and ask for advice about choices to be made. They could confess their faults knowing she would understand. Mary consoled and uplifted all those who knelt before her. You could watch from a distance and never grow tired of watching this "amazing grace."

And then, one day, the statue was gone. Someone had replaced this old worn statue of Mary with a modern one that fit in more tolerably with the décor. The new statue wasn't all that bad, but those who had knelt before the original one never felt the same. The essence of Mary had disappeared. Oh, people still knelt and prayed, but from a distance you could sense that something was missing; it was as if the magic had disappeared. Everyone wondered where had the other statue of Mary gone? Well, it went the way of all church artifacts that are no longer needed. It was placed in an ecumenical storehouse.

Now you would think this would be the end of the story, but there is more. There was a young man who lived with his sister in the South Bronx. He worked at the warehouse and quite unexpectedly came across the statue of Mary one day. By this time Mary really looked pretty worn and broken; but this young man had insight and saw the statue had potential. He asked his supervisor if it would be all right for him to restore the statue and place it in his neighborhood church. The parishioners of this small church in the South Bronx couldn't afford to purchase a new statue of Mary, but they never ceased praying that someday, by some miracle, they would acquire one.

The young man and his sister lived in a small house that had a basement which was used as a workshop. They were both natural born artists and enjoyed painting. Restoring the statue was a new challenge for them, and they looked forward to repairing Mary with great enthusiasm. To them, this did not seem like work. First, they washed the dirt and grime off the statue. The next step was to sand and re-plaster the parts that were broken.

Finally, Mary was ready for a new coat of paint. The colors they chose were soft and subtle; pale blue for her cape and sash; ivory for her gown; and sandals of gold to match her golden tiara. The most difficult part was painting Mary's face. It was important that she look beautiful, but natural. Tears came to their eyes as they gazed at the finished statue. She appeared lifelike! God had certainly inspired this brother and sister to restore his Mother in a most beautiful fashion. To both of them, restoring this statue did not seem at all like work. It was a pleasure to be enjoyed from start to finish and they were sorry to see the restoration come to an end.

On the feast of the Blessed Mother's birthday, September 8th, she was placed in the front of the church to the right of the altar. Mary had again found her home on Earth. How surprised the parishioners were to see this beautiful image of Mary! How the parishioners loved their statue and paid homage to their heavenly Mother. Once again, people came to kneel before her, to talk to her, to be comforted by her. After all, Mary is our Mother, and if you sit quietly in the back of a church where no one can see you, you also can observe from a distance the communion between Mother and child, for we are all her children and when we kneel before her, we too can be held spellbound!

Week Thirty-Six
Prayerful Reflection

My Children,

There is only one tragedy in life and that is to lose heaven. All that you suffer in this life – betrayals, broken relationships, illnesses – are hardships; not tragedies. But not aspiring to become a saint, that is a tragedy.

I will teach you to become saintly, but first you must spend time in the desert. You must surround yourselves with silence. Only then will you hear my voice and will I be able to teach you. Pray deeply in order that you may learn purity of heart and then you will be able to approach others in love.

You are the lamps I will use to light the world. You have heard me say: "Give bread to the hungry," but I tell you now: "To those who have bread, teach them to be hungry for me." I thirst for my people to become a holy nation, and you will be the instruments I shall use. Do not underestimate your value to me. I will use each and every one of you. Just let me hear you say, "Here I am Lord to do your will," and I will inspire and direct you. Let nothing disturb or frighten you. With me, all things are possible.

Week Thirty-Seven
Inspired Thought

Reflections on the World Trade Center Tragedy

Unless the Lord builds the house, those who build it labor in vain.
(Psalm 127:1)

When the World Trade Center was built, we thought those massive towers would last forever. The skill of the builders and the quality of the materials gave reason to believe this. However, on September 11, 2001, in only a few minutes, the work of many years crashed to the ground thereby demonstrating the fragility and impermanence of human structures.

History is filled with examples of once-towering achievements being destroyed in the aftermath of a natural calamity, war, or divine judgment. In the Old Testament, one of the most famous examples is the destruction of Solomon's temple in 586 B.C. by the Babylonians. It was a magnificent edifice that stood firm and strong for nearly four centuries. The temple was rebuilt and in 70 A.D. destroyed again.

In Egypt, we have examples of tombs, pyramids, statues and other remarkable accomplishments of man's skill; yet these too are becoming endangered because of deterioration caused by weather, pollution and time. They were built to last forever, but nothing material lasts forever, no matter how brilliantly and ingeniously it is made. Many other landmarks and historical buildings are also no more. We have only photographs and books to remind us that they ever existed.

In John 2:19, Jesus tells the Jews: "Destroy this temple and in three days I will build it up again." They retorted, "This temple took forty-six years to build and you are going to raise it up in three days!" Jesus was talking about the temple of his body. It was only after Jesus had been raised from the dead that his disciples understood the temple he was referring to was his body. They came to understand what the prophetic message in scripture and the words he had spoken to them truly meant.

In Corinthians 6:19, Saint Paul tells us that we are temples of the living God. We have been created in the image of God. We must remember only that which has been established and is maintained by God has permanence. Enemies may destroy our bodies, but cannot destroy our souls. Unless the Lord builds the house, its builders labor in vain. We are living temples that have been built by the Lord. We are indestructible. If we are found worthy, we too will be raised up, but until then we must spend our time on Earth doing good. Our temples must be beacons of light, drawing others to him. We have received this knowledge and love of him as a gift and, in turn, we must give this gift to others without cost. Thomas à Kempis said it so well: "If we seek our Lord Jesus in all things, we will truly find him; but if we seek ourselves, we will find ourselves, and that will be to our own great loss."

There is a poem written by Hattie Vose Hall which, to me, truly epitomizes the word "temple," and I would like to share it with you:

Two Temples

A Builder builded (sic) a temple,
He wrought it with grace and skill;
Pillars and groins and arches
All fashioned to work his will.
Men said, as they saw its beauty,
"It shall never know decay;
Great is thy skill, O Builder!
Thy fame shall endure for aye."

A Mother builded (sic) a temple
With living and infinite care,
Planning each arch with patience,
Laying each stone with prayer.
None praised her unceasing efforts,
None knew of her wondrous plan,
For the temple the Mother builded (sic)
Was unseen by the eyes of man.

Gone is the Builder's temple,
Crumpled into the dust;
Low lies each stately pillar,
Food for consuming rust.
But the temple the Mother builded (sic)
Will last while the ages roll,
For that beautiful unseen temple
Was a child's immortal soul.

It is reassuring when we realize that although hatred can destroy buildings of mortar and brick, it can never destroy the soul of a human that is built and nurtured upon love. Through his death and resurrection, Jesus has shown us that although it was possible for them to destroy the temple of his body they could not harm the temple of his soul. He has promised the same for us. During uncertain times in our lives such as these, remembering the promise of the resurrection should comfort and reassure us that no one can ever harm the unseen temple of our immortal soul.

Week Thirty-Seven
Prayerful Reflection

My Children,

Your city is in ruins, but it is also my city. I am aware of your suffering and pain. There is much confusion, but I tell you a new city will arise from the rubble – the City of God. It will be a new Jerusalem, built on the bones and blood of the martyrs who perished on that site. These people will not have died in vain. This land will become a holy land. All who pass through it will remember the damage that hatred and evil can do, but I will impress on their minds and hearts what love can do. I will teach them what can be accomplished when people reach out in harmony to help the least of my brethren.

Joy will fill their souls as they begin to restore your city. I will bless the work of their hands. It will be a work of love and become an example for others who have been victims of war to rebuild their cities and work together side by side to abolish discrimination. A kinder and gentler nation will arise from the ashes.

More important than the restoration of the land is that out of the ashes will come a new generation. Their bodies will be holy temples containing recreated hearts of love dwelling within them. This new generation will resemble the Ark of the Covenant. In the Old Testament, it was the Ark that held my holy word. I will use this new generation to contain a holy treasure: my word. They will be the Arks I will use to spread my word to all who do not know me.

Remember, the temple the builders erect, no matter how strong or magnificent, will eventually become dust; but the temple that God builds will last throughout the ages for it houses an immortal soul.

I will take much pleasure in watching this holy land once again become the land of the living. Be patient and do not be discouraged. All this will take time. First you will go through much hardship, but when your new city comes to pass, your God will be magnified and glorified. I am the God of Hosts and I invite you to be my guests at the restoration of this holy land.

"If my people who are called by my name, humble themselves, pray, seek my face, and turn from their wicked ways, then I will hear from heaven, forgive their sins, and heal their land."_(Chronicles 7:14)

Week Thirty-Eight
Inspired Thought

We Have Now Become Part of the World

They shall beat their swords into plowshares.
Nation shall not lift up sword against nation.
Neither shall they train for war anymore.
(Isaiah 2:4)

I would like to say something about September 11th, a day which will live in infamy. Gloria Steinem is known as a women's rights advocate. Although I may not always agree with her beliefs, she is often very insightful. After the unprovoked attack on American soil on 9/11, she made this statement: "We have now become part of the world." These are very profound words!

Before the tragedy, so many of us believed that we were not vulnerable to this form of attack. Americans have always felt very secure and protected in this land of ours. Prior to 9/11, it was thought that although this happened in other countries and nations – it would never happen in America. These evil events only happened in countries like Germany, where the Nazis took people out of their homes and exterminated them; in Cambodia, where people were killed because of ethnic cleansing, and in Africa where governments allowed children to starve. During our own involvement in World War I, World War II, Korea, and Vietnam, there was never such an attack on American soil. Since these conflicts were fought overseas, blood from these wars was not shed on American soil.

September 11th changed all that. This evil attack on the Twin Towers, a cowardly act in which many innocent victims were killed, awakened our country to the reality of international terrorism. It made us realize how it feels to have armed men at airports and checkpoints, and to be suspicious of others who don't exactly look like "Americans." We became part of the world. We now know what it feels like to be afraid. We are like other countries that are vulnerable to attack.

America may have its imperfections, but it is still the best place to live in the entire world. The people here have more opportunities and more chances of succeeding than anywhere else. It truly is the land of opportunity. As the song says, "If you can make it there, you can make it anywhere." America is a special place. God has blessed America, and continues to bless her.

Although it may be difficult to believe, some good did come out of the tragedy of 9/11. The American people pulled together, something we have always done when our freedom was being threatened. Policemen and firemen put aside their differences and worked side by side. Color became irrelevant as people across racial lines united to help one another. People lifted their eyes up to the heavens, attended mass, and prayed in their own way for strength and courage. All became one!

Maybe most importantly, it taught us compassion for the people in other countries who live under this threat daily. Maybe we have become more sympathetic to those who suffer. Maybe we opened our hearts as well as our pocketbooks to help the families of the victims. Maybe we realized that the world is a small place, and what we do for our brethren, we do for him who is our Father in heaven and for his Son, our brother, who showed us the way while he was on Earth. Maybe it made us understand the words Jesus spoke, "We are to be in the world, but not of the world."

We must never forget what occurred on September 11th. Let us especially remember that in the aftermath of what happened, we all became united as one!

Week Thirty-Eight
Prayerful Reflection

My Children,

Rise up from the ashes. Do away with things of the past that have sprung up in your life. They are from the evil one.

My light shines within you. My glory is upon you. You are a new creation. It is time for you not only to speak the word, but to become the word. I am commanding you to go forth, speaking the word in truth and showing the way of everlasting life to others.

Learn to be detached from anything that disturbs your peace. Avoid anything that causes anger or hate. Separate yourselves from possessions that obsess you or have control over you. Share generously with those who are less fortunate than you. Learn to do this, and I promise you a joy and peace that you have never experienced.

Enjoy life! There is no need for you to be anxious and afraid. I am with you. I am your strength. I am your courage. I am with you every moment of every day. No matter what you are doing, feel my presence.

This is the only way you will be able to cope with the problems that enter your life.

I want you to feel my presence in an intimate way. Only then, in every circumstance will you be filled with the peace that surpasses all understanding, and a joy that can only come from the knowledge that I am with you always.

You must fill yourself with my love. Then you must take the love I have filled you with and love others. This love is not of the world. It is a divine love! It will enable you to love others as the Father has loved you. This love will become a magnificent obsession and you will truly become a new creation.

Week Thirty-Nine
Inspired Thought

Through Acceptance, We Find Peace

Put things in order, listen to my appeal, accept one another, live in peace;
and the God of love and peace will always be with you.
(2 Corinthians: 13-14)

We should all pray: "God grant me the serenity to accept the things I cannot change, the courage to change the things I can, and the wisdom to know the difference." Some people are able to live by this philosophy; to accept whatever happens to them day by day without questioning the reason. Just as the earth, the sky and the seasons are part of the universe, to some people, things just are – no questions asked.

For others it is not easy to accept the world and the people who live in it as they are. God did not create us to be clones. He created each person to be an original; a tribute to God's creativity and so we should learn to celebrate our differences. If we are to truly love our neighbors as ourselves, it is necessary to accept people as they are and not demand they conform to our image. We are not made in the image of each other, but in God's image.

The writer Thoreau enlightened us by writing: "If we do not keep pace with our companions, perhaps it is because we hear a different drummer. We must step to the music that we hear, however measured or far away." Accept others who step to the music that they hear. We cannot discriminate against those who do not conform to our way of doing things.

During a trip to Florida, my friend and I started a conversation with a gentleman who was also waiting on line to be served. My friend made a comment on his "funny accent." The gentleman, looking my friend straight in the eye, said gently, but profoundly, "not funny, just different." Needless to say, we both learned a great lesson from this gentleman's wise statement. We realized that we humans have more in common than we have differences. The phrase, "We must learn to celebrate our differences if the human race is to survive!" became our motto. Although we cannot go back in time to correct all our past mistakes, but we can start from the present moment and make a new beginning.

God's world is perfect and orderly. In our humanness, we feel the need to put God's world in order, but instead we must put ourselves in order with God's world. How is this to be done? Through acceptance comes peace. Until we accept one another, we cannot live in peace. As humans we all experience the same things: we work, we eat, we cry, and we love. What makes us different is our backgrounds and how we do these things. When it is hard to accept certain people or situations, we should pray that God will give us a loving heart to see all of his children through his eyes. In loving, accepting and serving others, we will find peace, and love and happiness will be returned to us in abundance.

Week Thirty-Nine
Prayerful Reflection

My Children,

Cherish the moments you have with each other and with your loved ones. Your time on earth is precious and not to be wasted. Show and tell your loved ones how much they mean to you. Reconcile yourself with those who have trespassed against you. Forgive them! Make amends now! The time is short! Many of your loved ones, friends, acquaintances and enemies will soon be entering eternity.

Take the first step toward making peace. You will be setting an example, thereby helping others to make the same overture of reconciliation. Do not let pride or stubbornness stand in your way. When it comes to forgiveness, there is no right or wrong, no anger or hate, only love. Now is the time for healing, mercy, and love. Do not let this opportunity pass. You will be filled with much regret and guilt if you do not take the opportunity for closure. If you do your part and allow me to do mine, together we will achieve peace and harmony with all.

I wish to prepare a place for you at my banquet table, but if you do not heed my words and forgive, many seats will be left empty. At my table only peace, joy and love are seated. These virtues must reign in your heart if you are to sit and break bread with me. I invite you! Come! But you must reconcile all things here on earth before this can come to pass.

Week Forty
Inspired Thought

Here I Am, Lord!

Lord, to whom can we go? You have the words of eternal life!
(John 6:68)

How present are we to the voice of God? Do we easily understand what he wants from us? When he calls, do we recognize his voice? Parents can identify their child's voice and their children can recognize theirs, but this recognition only comes through intimacy. In 1 Samuel 3:1-10, we read how even God's chosen can readily mistake his voice:

> "One night Eli, whose eyes were becoming so weak that he could barely see, was lying down. The lamp of God had not yet gone out. Samuel was lying down in the temple of the Lord, where the Ark of God was. Then the Lord called Samuel. Samuel answered, 'Here I am,' and he ran to Eli and said, 'Here I am; you called me.' But Eli said, 'I did not call; go back and lie down.' So he went to lie down. Again the Lord called, 'Samuel!' And Samuel got up and went to Eli and said, 'Here I am; you called me.' 'My son,' Eli said, 'I did not call; go back

and lie down.' Now Samuel did not yet know the Lord: The word of the Lord had not yet been revealed to him. The Lord called Samuel a third time, and Samuel got up and went to Eli and said, 'Here I am, you called me.' Then Eli realized that the Lord was calling the boy. So Eli told Samuel, 'Go and lie down, and if he calls you, say, 'Speak, Lord, for your servant is listening.'"

This reading is critical because it reveals that it is only through intimacy with God that we come to recognize his voice. Even Samuel had to be taught this. At first, Samuel was not familiar with the Lord's voice. It was Eli who already had an intimate relationship with the Lord and recognized his voice. This is how it is with us. It takes time to recognize a once unfamiliar voice. The more time we spend with the Lord, the more we will recognize his voice and understand in what direction he is leading us.

In John 10:1-5, the words of Jesus confirm this to an even greater extent. The sheep hear the shepherd's voice. The shepherd calls his own by name and leads them. The sheep follow him because they recognize his voice. "I am the good shepherd. I know my sheep and my sheep know me in the same way that the Father knows me, and I know the Father. I have other sheep that do not belong to this fold. I must lead them too, and they shall hear my voice. There shall be one flock and one shepherd."

The image of God as our shepherd continues in the 23rd Psalm:

"The Lord is my shepherd, I shall not want. He makes me lie down in green pastures; He restores my soul. He leads me in right paths for his name's sake. Even though I walk through the darkest valley, I fear no evil; for you are with me; your rod and your staff they comfort me. You prepare a table before me in the presence of my enemies; you anoint my head with oil; my cup overflows. Surely goodness and mercy shall follow me all the days of my life, and I shall dwell in the house of the Lord my whole life long."

The belief that God as a guardian and comforter in our lives is something we desperately hunger to believe, and Psalm 23 expresses that desire magnificently.

The truth is we are all vulnerable, not only to danger and misfortune, but also to temptation, fear, doubt, and selfishness. We're vulnerable like sheep being led astray and to following forces that can destroy our lives or turn us from our families, friends and neighbors. We're vulnerable to the superficial trappings that we think will protect us – our possessions, reputation, and pride – but these things do no more to protect us than the sheep's fluffy white wool.

Only Christ can guide us and protect us when we are helpless and in need, but how can he help us in our need if we do not hear his voice? In Isaiah 53:6-7, we read the description of the suffering servant: "We all, like sheep, have gone astray; each of us has turned to his own way, and the Lord has laid on himself the iniquity of us all. He was oppressed and afflicted, yet he did not open his mouth; he was led like a lamb to the slaughter and as a sheep before his shearers in silence, and he did not open his mouth."

Isaiah's description is a prophecy of Christ's crucifixion. Jesus is the Lamb who took upon himself the sins of us all, suffering in silence on our behalf. How vividly these words invoke the last hours of Jesus and his willing, unresisting death at the hands of his enemies! The cross makes us aware of the intimacy between Jesus and his Father. He became the Lamb who heard the voice of his Father and obeyed! In him, we have a shepherd who sets the perfect example of trust in his Father. We must also learn to listen to his voice, and to trust him when we are weak and helpless, otherwise, we will fail in whatever we attempt.

Let us hope and pray that we will always recognize his voice when he calls out to us, and that we will always willingly reply: "Here we are, Lord! Make of us what pleases you. We come to do your will!"

Week Forty
Prayerful Reflection

My Children,

You have a mission! I am sending you forth as a light to the nations. You must help others to believe that I am from the Father. You must help others to understand that when they look at my image, hear my name, or read of me, that I am sent from the Father. How else will others come to know that there is a God and that heaven truly exists? Only when you reveal to those who do not know me what I have told you, will my people begin to live in peace and harmony. If all my people truly believed in God, do you think they would act toward one another the way they do? Do you think there would be such hatred, brother fighting against brother, in all parts of the world? Look around! Don't you see all the sinful things that are occurring in the world today? With their lips they say they believe, but their hearts are far from me.

There is much to do! My mission while on Earth was to give glory to the Father. That mission is to continue through you. Help others to believe. They must believe that "I AM" exists. Only then will they come to understand that "I AM" sent me, his only beloved Son, to give life that changes but never ends. They must look upon my countenance and see my Father, the Creator of all things. They must look upon me and see the power of my Spirit, the Re-Creator, who makes all things new.

In order for you to accomplish this mission, it is necessary for you to put aside your egos and hurts. Do not dwell on your past mistakes or failures. What is done cannot be undone. Do not analyze my expectations of you. My ways are not your ways.

I have always chosen the weak things of the world to accomplish my work. I will use each and every one of you according to your gifts. I ask only one thing of you. You must draw closer to me. Listen to my voice. I will direct you. You have read my word many times. You have heard it spoken many times. Those who believe that my word is true, that he sent me, his only beloved Son, to give eternal life, must go forth and proclaim what I have revealed to them. Go forth and reveal my message to those who do not know me. Teach others to seek the truth. The world and all that is in it will be changed in the twinkling of an eye. All you do for the least of my brethren you do for me, and I love you dearly for all your sacrifices.

Remember, it was not nails that held me to the cross, but my love for you. You must have that love for one another. Blessed are those who have not seen – yet believe. You have been chosen by me because you believe!

Week Forty-One
Inspired Thought

How Long Must I Be with You?

They asked, "Are you saying we are blind?
Jesus answered, "If you were blind, you wouldn't be guilty, but your guilt
remains because you claim to know what you are doing."
(John 9:41)

When the Son of Man walked the Earth, he said to us, "How long must I be with you before you see?" We said, "He's crazy. Crucify him. He's an extremist," but we tolerated him. He continued to say, "How long must I be with you before you see?" We answered, "He's eccentric," but we rather liked him and smiled at him. He stubbornly asked again, "How long must I be with you, before you see?" Then we said, "There might be something in what he is saying. Let us give him half an ear." He again asked the question, "How long must I be with you before you see?"

Finally, our eyes and hearts were opened and we did see, and we gathered around him to listen to his word. We understood what he said to us and we felt the need to do something in gratitude for what he gave us. We asked him, "What can we do to express our regret in taking so long to understand?" He touched us with the tips of his fingers and kissed us. We asked, "How can we repay you? We were so slow in understanding the truth. Will you ever forgive us?" Jesus replied, "What can you do? Nothing more than you have done. The important thing is that you now see! That is reward enough. You see!" It is true. We can shout to all we meet, "Our eyes have been opened. We see! And if you follow him, you too will see the glory of God!" Now, when Jesus asks us as he did Simon Peter, "Who do you say I am?" We can answer as Peter did, "You are the Messiah – the Son of the living God." And Jesus will respond to us in the same way he did to Peter, "Blest are you, for no mere man has revealed this to you, but my heavenly Father." (Matthew 16:15-18)

If we put God first, then our relationship with others is built on a sound basis and everything else falls into place. At the start of each year, we make new resolutions hoping to better ourselves, our lives, and our circumstances; but somehow we fall short every year. Maybe we don't succeed in most of the things we try to accomplish because we are not depending on him. We are trying to do it on our own. It is only through prayer, building a strong relationship with him, and putting his kingdom first that we will understand his will for us and the direction in which he is leading us. God came to Earth as Jesus to bless us with his human voice. They killed our Lord, but they could not kill the word. Two thousand years later, his word is still spoken. He instructs us: "Seek first the kingdom, and all things shall be given unto you." He who has started this great work in us will complete it. When we are weak, he is strong, and we can do all things through him who strengthens us.

If we are to see and understand, we must realize that God reveals himself to us not only through scripture readings but through things in our everyday lives such as books, music, people, and nature. It is no coincidence that God reveals his word through all those things he created for us to enjoy! Therefore when we connect with the written words of a book or article, or when the lyrics of song that we hear touch us, or when someone utters a phrase that inspires us, we should not assume that it is by chance. If we allow ourselves to be open to it, we will realize that it is through the power of the Holy Spirit that we receive this message. The idea that God would reveal himself and his holy word to us using the ordinary and common makes perfect sense. Jesus became ordinary and common, human, in order to make his Father and his word known to us. Why wouldn't God continue to work through the common and ordinary things of the world to continue to speak to us, reveal his word and make himself known to us? God makes known to us his living word through the stuff of life.

May God always keep our eyes open to see him and to reveal himself through the things and people around us! May we always hear how he is calling us! And may we never hear him ask: "How long must I be with you before you finally see?

Week Forty-One
Prayerful Reflection

My Children,

Your soul is worth more than all the gold in the world, worth more than all the power of the world's leaders, worth more than all the knowledge in all the libraries of the world. Your soul is worth more than anything in the world that you might possess. That is why I sent my Son Jesus, on a specific day to a specific place on Earth's map to be born. Divine love came to Earth that day! Ever since that moment, there is no us; no them. We are all one. You are all sisters and brothers of my Son, and I am your Father.

Children of the light must reach out to those in darkness and reverse the trend toward moral decay. Emphasize what is positive and virtuous. Look for the good in one another. I have given you the power to heal minds, hearts, and souls. The greatest example you can give is to love one another. Teach my children that when moral laws are broken, the price is inner turmoil and suffering; when my commandments are obeyed, the reward is peace and joy.

When my Son finished his life on Earth, he had not fed everyone; he had not solved all the problems of the world. Yet he completed the work I called him to do. This is what I ask of you. Search your hearts and pray to the Holy Spirit for guidance to finish the work I have called you to complete. The power of my Holy Spirit will aid you. Reach out to those in need, using the gifts with which you have been blessed.

To do this, it is important that in all circumstances you keep hope alive. To hope is to have faith and belief in what you do not see and do not understand. Have patience. Many situations will become worse before they get better. When it is difficult for you to see the light at the end of the tunnel, it will be hope that will get you through. In the end, faith, hope and love remain – so be of good hope! When your work on Earth is finished, your reward will be great and I will bless you with the words: "Well done, good and faithful servant!"

When you come to the realization that life is not so much a problem to be solved as a mystery to be lived; it will set you free. The human journey is so short. You no sooner realize that you are here when it is already time for you to be leaving. In life there is both sorrow and joy. Sorrow does not come from me. It comes from the choices my children make during their journey on Earth. I created you to experience the full measure of my joy. My gift to you, if you keep my commandments, is that your cup of joy will overflow.

There are many pleasures on Earth that I have created just for your enjoyment and happiness, and you will be held accountable for denying yourself any of the joys that life has to offer during your stay. The secret of life is enjoying the passage of time. Do not waste time in fear, which is useless. Use the time you have left wisely, doing good works. This will prepare a place in eternity for you. Time is as valuable as eternity because it is through time on earth that God and heaven are reached.

Week Forty-Two
Inspired Thought

He Has Forgiven Us

The laws are good when used as God intended.
(1 Timothy 1:8)

We hear of many courtroom dramas taking place. Every time we open a newspaper, we read of someone being accused of some horrendous act. The accused is put on trial and found to be guilty or not guilty by a jury of twelve. If found guilty, the accused is punished; if found innocent, set free.

With God as our judge, things work differently. We are continually being forgiven, which of course, implies that we are guilty. Yet our crimes are not counted because of the death and resurrection of our Savior who paid the debt for our sins. Therefore, we always receive a verdict of "not guilty!"

Christ shed his blood to cancel the guilt of our crimes. Righteousness does not come from the law, but comes from faith in Christ. Christ's death and resurrection have become the basis for our pardon and our perfection. Christ died for the unrighteous as well as the righteous in order to unite all with the Father. Christ's death not only paid for our salvation, but is also intended to draw us closer to God. "He who did not spare his own Son but gave him up for all of us, how will he not also graciously give us all things?" (Romans 8:32) What does "give us all things" mean? He will give us all things that are good for us - all things we need to be conformed to the image of his Son; all things to obtain everlasting joy.

We will be able to do all things through him who strengthens us. Because of the sacrifice of our loving Savior Jesus, the burdens we carry in life will never be as heavy as the chains from which we were set free.

Week Forty-Two
Prayerful Reflection

My Children,

I can recall each and every time you were hurt and betrayed, and who was responsible. I saw how it affected your life. Bring that hurt to me.

I will bless your hurt and transform your suffering with my love. I will wipe away all your tears and you will never again let yourself be disturbed by those who hurt you bodily or mentally. The disappointments in your life will be transformed through the power of my Holy Spirit and you will bear much fruit.

Never forget that I love those who hurt you as much as I love you. Do not be bitter and angry at others. Be kind and merciful toward all. But most of all, forgive, forgive, forgive! I know you have heard these words over and over again, but the true way to happiness is to love and to forgive. By your example of forgiveness you will draw many to me.

Pray for guidance and strength and I will honor your prayer. I promise you a peace and joy that you have never known.

I am your fortress, your place of safety. Do what is right and just in my sight and remember that in the end, it is only the soul that matters. Never put yourself in a situation that would cause you to lose your soul. You are too precious in my sight!

I wish to make you a saint!

Week Forty-Three
Inspired Thought

Store up Heavenly Treasure

But this precious treasure –
this light and power that now shines within us –
is held in a perishable container, that is, in our weak bodies.
Everyone must see that this glorious power
is from God and is not our own.
(2 Corinthians 4:7-9)

"Withdraw your heart from the world before God takes your body from it." These are the words of St. John of Avila, and they are the words that saints are able to live by. Little by little, they detach their hearts from worldly possessions and as their worldly desires decrease, their love and knowledge of God increases. Saints are in the world, but they are not of the world. Saints have always had the wisdom to know that we are born into time, but at death we are born into eternity. Whenever St. Teresa of Avila heard the clock ticking, she thanked God because it reminded her that she was just that much closer to entering heaven. From the minute we set foot on this planet, our lives are controlled by the ticking of the clock and sooner or later, time runs out for each one of us.

When Jesus taught us the Our Father he said: "Thy kingdom come, thy will be done on Earth as it is in heaven." God's will reigns in heaven. There are no exceptions. Saints, out of love for the Lord, wish only to do God's will. For them, "thy kingdom come" has already come on Earth.

Our entering the kingdom depends on how obedient we are to the Father's will. Our God is such a just and merciful God, and we are all equal in his eyes. He is the master of equality. On Earth, we fight for equality in the workplace, equality between the sexes, and equality among the races, but only in God is there true equality. He does not say to us, "Because you are beautiful, or rich or smart, you will enter heaven." We must never do anything on Earth that would jeopardize our entering the kingdom. We are created for eternity! We must never do anything on Earth which will separate us from the love of God! God forbid we should ever do anything to endanger our salvation! Let us always have the fervor of the saints who understood that we must "Seek first the kingdom of God and trust that all else will be added." (Matthew 6:33)

In the gospels, Jesus tells us about the kingdom. He spurs our interest by giving us clues as to what the kingdom will be: "In my Father's house, there are many mansions," and "Eye has not seen, nor ear heard what my Father has prepared." As I contemplated these words, two parables came to mind. The first from Matthew 13:44, is about a farmer who comes across a treasure while digging in a field. He then buries the treasure and goes home to sell all that he has so he can buy the field. Once he owns that field, the treasure will legally be his. In the second parable from Matthew 13:45, a merchant did exactly what the farmer had done: he sells all that he owns in order to purchase a "pearl of great price." Both men's hearts were filled with the desire to obtain earthly treasure.

We all have the desire to obtain earthly treasure and many of us can relate to these parables. I remember when my husband, mother, and sister saw our house for the first time. We pooled all our money and were able to manage the down payment. Like the farmer and the merchant, to us this house was both the hidden treasure in the field and the pearl of great price. This house was to become our home for the next 50 years and we have enjoyed the protection and comfort it has provided us with for all these past years. But looking back, I realize the true treasures are the wonderful memories of love and affection that we shared in our home. In Matthew 6:19-22, Jesus instructs us: "Store up treasure in heaven, that which moth and rust cannot destroy, for where your treasure is, there your heart will also be." He is enlightening us to have greater fervor for spiritual treasures than for earthly possessions. To possess heaven is the greatest treasure! God has given us the world and its possessions to use and enjoy, but never at the risk of losing the kingdom. "What doth it profit a man if he gains the whole world yet lose his soul?" (Matthew 16:26)

Two of the most frequently used words in the Catholic faith are: "saecula, saeculorum," which translated mean "forever and ever." We should aspire to have earthly houses for our short stay in our earthly kingdom, but our greatest desire should be to live in the house of the Lord forever and ever! Amen!

Week Forty-Three
Prayerful Reflection

My Children,

I have given you many precious gifts, but the one I treasure is the gift of time. Value this precious gift! Use it wisely! Take notice, my dear children, that your whole lives are composed of minutes, hours, and days that pass by so rapidly. Look up at the clouds, the same clouds on which the Son of Man will return, and see how swiftly they move on a windy day. Let them remind you of how time is fleeting. Your portion of time on this earth is fast disappearing.

The way you spend your time is a witness before God. The deeds that you do will either testify for you or against you. You have the freedom of choice – either to make good or bad use of your lifetime. Time that has passed will never return. All the wealth, all the tears that ever flowed cannot purchase one single moment of past time.

A torn garment can be mended, a destroyed edifice can be rebuilt, a defeated army can be gathered together to win a victory, but time once lost is gone forever. Time is what life is made of. Each lifetime has its share of tragedy and unhappiness, but just as time passes so will hardships also pass.

Remember, you are a resurrection people and are not of this world. Events and situations should not discourage you or cause you to despair. Remain focused on your journey towards eternity. The evil one is cunning. He knows when you feel vulnerable and that is the time he attacks. His mission is for you to become discouraged, to give up hope, and so let us pray: "Lord, always guide us in making the correct decisions according to your holy will, and may we never desire to possess anything that would endanger our salvation. Amen!"

Week Forty-Four
Inspired Thought

Thank God, We're Free at Last!

Search me, O God, and know my heart; test me and know my thoughts.
See if there is any wicked way in me, and lead me in the way everlasting.
(Psalm 139:23)

I remember going to church on the feast of St. Vincent and as I received Communion from the priest, I realized the wafer was part of the host broken at the Consecration. I have always felt kind of special when I receive that piece of the Body of Christ! I went back to my seat to offer up my communion for people whom I felt needed it that day and I started to pray very deeply. Through the Holy Spirit's inspiration, the word "freedom" entered into my thoughts, and with it, the discernment to understand that I have the freedom not to let others invade my joy.

There are mornings when I wake up thinking it is going to be a pretty good day, but then someone says a word to upset me, or something goes wrong and my day is ruined. But sitting in church that day, the truth hit me; I have the freedom of choice. If I allow others to disillusion me, or depress me, or bring me down, I have only myself to blame. Maybe

I am getting what I deserve because I have a tendency to involve myself in issues that really do not concern me. Am I guilty of trying to solve everyone's problems? I must learn to "Let go and let God!"

The words spoken in John 21:20-22, came to my mind: "Peter asked Jesus, 'Lord, what about him?' Jesus answered, 'What concern is he of yours?'" In other words, "Peter, mind your own business! You have enough on your plate." He may just as well be speaking to me when I concern myself with affairs that are none of my business. We are obligated to help one another, but we cannot always expect to be successful in saving our family, our friends, the nation, the world. We mean well and have good intentions, but sometimes we interfere to the extent that we become obnoxious, and turn others off. It is during these times we should remember that we have the freedom to back off and trust that God is in control.

We are always trying to mold others into what we think they should be or permit others to mold us into what they think we should be. We forget that we are all made in the image of God, and he is the only one who can fashion and mold us into a one-of-a-kind specialty. We are doing a grave injustice to God's plans for others when we try to take over and control them, and we must never permit others to dissuade us from the way God is leading us.

Freedom also allows us to understand that we must not worry about what others think of us. We are fearful that we will upset others if we do not give in to their expectations of what we should say or do. This is wrong! Loving or being loved is based on a relationship that casts out fear. We must act justly toward our neighbor, walk humbly, and love tenderly. This is what our Lord asks of us.

God wants us to be independent, confident Christians. We have been freed from the chains of oppression and bondage. Christ paid heavily for our freedom, and we must never put ourselves in chains again. We must never again allow others to have control over us or to manipulate us. Free at last! Thank God, we are free at last!

Week Forty-Four
Prayerful Reflection

My Children,

I wish to tell you one of the secrets of having a life filled with joy! You have not lived fully until you have done something for someone who can never repay you. The greatest joy that you can experience is to do a service for someone in secret, and then without revealing it, have that person discover it was you. It will not be by accident that they will uncover your good deeds. It will be because I who see what you do in secret wish to reward you, and so I have revealed your good works to them. Work in secret and allow me to reveal to others that the reason they have benefited is because of your good works. This is the true meaning of a joyful giver. I will bless you abundantly because you are rendering your service out of love and not out of duty. As a result, your heart will be overflowing with a joy that is not of this world.

It is not always easy to be obedient to my will, but I promise you, I will give you courage and strength to face the difficult tasks that I set before you. I will give you sufficient grace for all the challenges that come your way. I will instill in you the patience and understanding you need to serve those I put before you. I am depending on you as there is much work for you to do in the coming days, but you will not find it difficult, because I have revealed to you the secret of being successful in whatever you attempt to accomplish. Do your work in secret! Do not look for thanks and praise from those you serve. I, your Father, who sees what you do in secret, will reward you greatly!

Week Forty-Five
Inspired Thought

Seeing Others through the Eyes of Jesus

Love your neighbor as yourself.
Love does no wrong to a neighbor;
therefore, love is the fulfilling of the law.
(Romans 13:9)

I once read a book called <u>Abounding Grace</u>, an anthology of wisdom. Some of the reflections were titled: Happiness; Courage; Compassion; Faith; and Goodness.

The chapter titled 'Respect' was so enlightening that I would like to share it with you.

"During the war with Japan, an American psychiatrist working in a Japanese hospital wrote an article dealing with respect: 'One day I received a call from my superior that there was a stark naked and raving mental patient in the cleaning closet. He was scaring all the Japanese cleaning women who were running around in a panic. I was the psychiatrist on duty that day. I reached the floor where all the chaos was taking place and talked the man into coming out of the closet. I instructed the nurses to put him back into his room under supervision. The Japanese women were so appreciative they started to bow before me, kissing my hand and thanking me in Japanese. This episode taught me to have the greatest respect for these women. I realized that for the two years I worked in this hospital I had never noticed these hard working cleaning women; had never once said "hello" to them or acknowledged them in any way. I was oblivious to them. I did not do this because I am a rude man. I honestly never noticed them. I was too busy. They had their job to do and I had mine. I never thought it very important to take the time to understand these women or what it meant to walk in their shoes. But the lesson I learned was that if all these cleaning women were to quit their jobs, the hospital wouldn't function efficiently. They were important and they deserved to be noticed, to be respected, and to be thanked for a job well done.'"

Respect comes from the word 'spectacle'. It means not only to look, but to see things of importance. To take the blindness from our eyes, we must be alert, but this is not always the case. We must learn to see others through the eyes of Jesus. The words Saint Paul wrote in 1 Corinthians 9:19-23 come to mind: "For though I am free with respect to all, I have made myself a slave to all, so that I might win more of them. To the Jews, I became as a Jew, in order to win them. To those under the law, I became as one under the law (though I myself am not under the law) so that I might win those under the law. To those outside the law I became as one outside the law (though I am not free from God's law but am under God's law) so that I might win those outside the law. To the weak I became weak, so that I might win the weak. I have become all things to all people that I might by all means save some. I do it all for the sake of the gospel, so that I may share in its blessings."

Although we were all created in God's same image, we are all not the same. Any parent will tell you that although their children may have the same father and mother, each child is different and unique in looks, personality and temperament. So it is with the children of God. We are different. Different looks. Different personalities. Different temperaments. Different genders. Different races. Different religions. Different sexual preferences. Paul is telling us that despite these differences, love and tolerance is possible. When Paul became "all things to all people" he temporarily put himself in their place. Yet he did not become something he was not. He still spoke the truth, but his insight into the plight of others helped him to tell the truth with loving kindness and not anger. Not only were people able to better to relate to Paul, he was better able to relate to them, because by putting himself in their situation, he was minimizing the differences between them. He became more open to accepting them and they became open to accepting him. When we put aside our differences we are more open to learning from others and they are more open to learning from us.

Like Paul, we do all this for the sake of the gospel. But what a lesson in human relations Paul has given us! Understanding and respecting of another's point of view is a very wise way of communicating and often it leads to more peaceful and quicker resolutions. How much our relationships would improve if we practiced Paul's technique of being open to other's viewpoints while staying true to our own. Learning to respect and embrace differences will help us solve problems that we come across in our family, circle of friends and community. If we are having a confrontation with someone we love, temporarily putting ourselves in their shoes and offering them respect helps us to take the blindness from our eyes so that we can deal with situations in ways that God would want us to.

Jesus was able to look into the hearts of his people and that is why he could advise them so efficaciously, compassionately, and mercifully. Let us see others through his eyes!

Week Forty-Five
Prayerful Reflection

My Children,

When you look around, you hear and see signs of people's suffering and pain. Yet, you have become somewhat detached and immune to all that surrounds you. Maybe this avoidance is your way of dealing with the brutal acts that are occurring.

Be of good faith. Do not be afraid. I am with you. I know that each one of you has personal demons to fight – sickness, betrayals and trials in your own lives that you must deal with. What does it matter what you lose in life, as long as I remain? I will comfort you and instill in you courage so that you will be able to overcome any evil that comes to you or your family.

I have chosen you, and you have responded to my call, but this is not enough. You know me personally, and this is a blessing that will remain with you always. Now I am pleading for you to reach out and help those who are in greater need. There are those who do not know me. They do not have me to lean on. Do not forsake them. I have asked you to turn your cheek; not your back. Each person's suffering affects you because you are all part of my body. You must reach out, have compassion, and heal their wounds and brokenness. Learn to trust me completely and you will not fail in reaching out to help those in need. You have me! They need me.

Because you have the faith to believe in what you do not see, they will come to see me through your faith. You are precious in my sight and whatever you do for the least of my brethren, you do for me. All are precious in my sight, and I will never forget any kindness that you show to any of my broken-hearted children.

Week Forty-Six
Inspired Thought

A Vision of Hallowed Halls

In my Father's house there are many dwelling places.
If it were not so, would I have told you
that I go to prepare a place for you?
(John 13:2)

With the Holy Spirit as my guide, I entered the wonderful Temple of Christianity.

I started at the door of Genesis and walked through the Old Testament Art Galleries where the pictures of Noah, Abraham, Moses, Joseph, Jacob and Daniel hung on the wall.

I entered the Music Room of Psalms where the Holy Spirit played a hymn on God's great organ and I heard the tuneful harp of David, the sweet singer of Israel.

I strolled into the Chamber of Ecclesiastes where I heard the voice of the preacher, Qoheleth, and sweet-scented spices filled my life.

I then opened the door of the Business Office of Proverbs and noticed the Observatory Room of the Prophets where I saw telescopes pointed to the hills of Judea, where my salvation took place.

I entered the Audience Room of the King of Kings and caught a vision of his glory as told in the gospels of Matthew, Mark, Luke and John.

I walked into the Chamber of the Acts of the Apostles where the Holy Spirit was doing his work in the formation of the infant church.

Then I turned into the Correspondence Room of Peter, Paul, James and John and watched as they prepared the Epistles.

I stepped into the Throne Room of Revelation and caught a vision of the King of Glory sitting at the right hand of the Father.

I saw all these things and knelt down in praise and thanksgiving to the Holy Spirit for opening my heart to see all these wondrous things. Now I am filled with the power of this same Spirit through whom I can do all things, for the mysteries of God's kingdom have been revealed to me!

Week Forty-Six
Prayerful Reflection

My Children,

Your love of Jesus should draw you to visit him often in the tabernacle. You shall find supreme happiness as you kneel in prayer before him at the foot of the altar; you shall find the courts of the Lord most attractive; you shall cry out with the prophets, "How lovely are thy tabernacles, O Lord of Hosts!" But alas, how often is the place where my Son dwells left alone. The palaces of earthly kings, princes, and the rich are filled with visitors who pay them homage, but where my Son is, there is no one. Shall the palace of the King of Kings and Lord of Lords be deserted and forgotten? How my Son longs for you to visit him, but it is to no avail. The church is empty. He sits alone.

Jesus is there on the altar to welcome all, to bestow his grace on all, yet few come to receive his gifts. Taste and experience the sweetness of the love of my Son in the tabernacle, and you will remember these moments as the happiest times of your life. Blessed are they who dwell in the house of the Lord, praising him forever and ever!

My saints knew the benefit that came from adoring my Son in the Eucharist. While on Earth, Saint Paschal was watching his sheep on the mountainside when he heard the consecration bells ring out from a church in the valley below, where the villagers had assembled for mass. Saint Paschal immediately stopped what he was doing out of respect, and started to pray. One of my angels, bearing in his hands the Sacred Host, appeared to Saint Paschal, who immediately fell on his knees in adoration. Learn from this holy saint. He will teach you how it pleases me when you pay homage to my Son in the Eucharist. The Blessed Sacrament, the Body and Blood of my Son Jesus, is to you a mystery, but the more you visit him as he waits in the tabernacle, the more you will come to understand. The presence of Jesus in the Eucharist fulfills his promise: "I will not leave you orphans!"

Week Forty-Seven
Inspired Thought

Reflections on the Book, <u>The Purpose Driven Life</u>

God does not play dice with the universe!
(Albert Einstein)

In the film, <u>Chariots of Fire</u>, the minister feels compelled to run in the Olympics, but his family and church feel God is calling him to be a missionary in China. He feels the urging of the Holy Spirit and he tells his sister, "This is something I must do. God gave me the ability to run fast for a purpose; for his purpose, and when I run it is for God's glory, and when I win, it is for God's glory."

God has created each of us for a specific purpose. The following excerpt is from <u>The Purpose Driven Life</u>, by Rick Warren:

"God's purpose for our life is far greater than our own personal fulfillment, peace of mind, or happiness. Our purpose in life is greater than our families, careers, or ambitions. If we want to know why we were placed on this planet, we must begin with God. We were born by his purpose and for his purpose. We ask questions like what do I want to be? What should I do with my life? What are my dreams for the future? But focusing on ourselves will never reveal life's purpose. The Bible says, "It is God who directs the lives of his creatures – everyone's life is in his power." You did not create yourself, so there is no way you can tell yourself what you were created for. If you were handed an invention you had never seen before, you wouldn't know its purpose. Only the creator or the owner's manual could reveal its purpose. God is our creator and only He can reveal our purpose in life. We were made by God and for God, and until we all understand that, life will never make any sense.

God was thinking of us long before we ever thought about him. His purpose for our lives predates our conception. He planned it before we existed, without our input. We may choose our career, our spouse, our hobbies, and many other parts of our life, but we don't get to choose our purpose. The purpose of our life fits into a much larger cosmic purpose that God has designed for eternity. It is no accident that we are alive and breathing this moment. God wanted to create us. He deliberately chose our race, the color of our skin, hair and other features. He custom made our bodies just the way he wanted. He also determined the natural talents we would possess and the uniqueness of our personality. God knows us inside and out. Because God made us for a reason, He decided when we would be born and how long we would live. God left no detail to chance. He planned it for his purpose. Children may be unplanned by their parents, but they are not unplanned by God. He was thinking of us even before he made the world. God designed this planet's environment just so we could live in it.

Why did God do all this? Why did he bother to go to all the trouble of creating a universe for us? He did it because he is a

God of love. This kind of love is difficult to fathom, but it is a fundamental truth. We were created as a special manifestation of God's love. God made us so he could love us. This is a truth to build our lives on."

God did not create us just to live on this planet. We must never lose sight of his purpose for each and every one of us – no matter how successful we are during our earthly lives. We are created to live eternally with him. "What doth it profit a man's soul if he were to gain the whole world, but lose eternity?" (Matthew 16:26)

Week Forty-Seven
Prayerful Reflection

My Children,

I have made you far more wondrous than you could ever comprehend. You do not recognize all the talents I have given you. Do you wish to understand how you are to serve me? Give yourself to me this day and every day, and I will use you to bring my tender and compassionate work to others. You need not be aware of the work you do in my name nor worry about the outcome. It is enough for you to know that you are my servant, a tool in my hand, and you are deeply loved by me. I am continually shaping and molding you to be the person I created you to be, and it is only when you are called to eternal life, that you will be completed.

I know all you do for me and how hard you try to please me. You must not despair if events turn out differently than you planned. The evil one is cunning and tries to turn your love into hate and your compassion into bitterness by surrounding you with those who seek to discourage and make you seem less worthy than you are. Do not take notice of what others say or think of you. You are precious in my sight.

That is why I am sending you forth as my gift to the world to bring new life to those who are in darkness. You are to share the warmth, tenderness and protection of my love with those who are downtrodden, ill, and depressed. Especially seek out those whom you dislike because they have betrayed you and caused you harm. This is the most difficult task of all, for it is easy to love those who love you, but not easy to love your enemies. How often have I heard the phrase, "God, I am only human; what can I do?" Remember that I, your God, am both human and divine. All you need do is plant the seed and I will do the work.

It is not by accident that I chose you. Each one of you has been uniquely created by me, and the good I have begun in you will continue to the day of fruition. I bless your comings and goings abundantly because you are willing to serve me and to share me with those who are in darkness.

Rejoice in each other! Enjoy each other's uniqueness! You are all of vital importance to me. Use the gifts that I have given you to go forth in love and show others that I am a God of love and mercy. I wish to be one with them as I am one with you. Share with them your experiences and how knowing me intimately has changed your life. By this simple act, you will lead many souls to believe that I AM. I am your shepherd. Be still. Pray deeply. You will hear my voice and I will instruct you. Be of good courage. I am with you.

Week Forty-Eight
Inspired Thought

The Girl Who Used to Be Me!

Follow your bliss!
(Joseph Campbell)

Have you ever looked in the mirror and asked yourself, "What happened to the girl who used to be me?" In the film, <u>Shirley Valentine</u>, this is the question that Shirley keeps asking herself. Shirley is married and has two grown children. Her whole life revolves around her family. All the hopes and dreams of her youth have disappeared. She has now become the wife, the mother, the cook, and the housekeeper. Then a friend wins a trip for two to Greece and invites Shirley to accompany her. Shirley sums up enough courage to go and during these two weeks, she falls in love with Greece and finds the Shirley Valentine she used to be.

This movie came to mind after I ran into a friend of mine whom I hadn't seen in many years. We started chatting and after we said goodbye, I felt disturbed. This friend had remembered me very well. She had reminded me of all the passions, dreams, and interests of my youth. She had asked me, "Did I still…? Did I ever do anything about it? Am I still…?" Sadly I answered, "No!" to all her questions. All the wonderful things I thought I would accomplish had never come to be. I realized that all my ambitions of long ago were unfulfilled. Something was missing in my life and it was me. Since I became the wife, the mother, the cook, the housekeeper, I was no longer me. I had displaced myself with the needs and wants of my family. Some nights, lying in bed, I was unable to sleep because my heart and head were filled with the needs of others; I started to feel like Shirley Valentine. What about my wants and needs? I never regretted being a wife and a mother, but to have lost my identity so completely was wrong, and I had only myself to blame. I had let it happen by not taking the time to pursue my own interests.

I remember reading about a harried housewife who compared herself to a large stove. On the front burners were huge pots and pans filled to the brim and boiling over. These were the people who called on her day and night for service. They wanted her all, and she was always at their beck and call. They demanded her constant attention. On the back burner was a little saucepan which you could hardly see and she felt this was her. She had put aside all her dreams, all the things she cared about to tend to the needs of others. Not once did anyone concern themselves with her goals, her ambitions. To them, her dreams didn't matter. To them, it was as if she didn't exist. She had become invisible. She was there for one purpose and one purpose only: to fulfill the needs of others.

Suddenly, after reading that story, I saw the light! The realization of it hit me hard. I had become that little saucepan. At that moment, I made a very important decision in my life. I decided to give myself the gift of one year. I was going to search my heart, mind, and soul for something I really enjoyed doing and for one year, each day, I was going to make sure I spent time doing it.

I made a commitment to spend at least thirty minutes every day in silence. During this time I would read a spiritual book or just sit quietly. Once I began, enlightening ideas started to invade my inner thoughts, and as I wrote them down, I discovered I had a talent for expressing myself on paper. My writings are a result of my gift to myself. The most wonderful part of giving yourself this gift is that it restores and changes you. Your attitude toward others is different because you don't feel short-changed any longer.

A promise to this commitment will yield an amazing result. Life takes on new meaning when you are doing something creative. You realize it's not selfish to enjoy doing that which gives you pleasure. Your happiness is contagious to those around you and they also benefit. God has blessed each of us with our own individual talents and we should put these talents to good use so that we will not be in danger of losing them. Therefore, it is necessary that we take the time to explore ourselves, to search for our hidden talents, and to rediscover "the girl or boy, young woman or young man, that used to be me."

I suggested this gift of one year to an acquaintance who acknowledged to me that she was feeling worthless, as if her life were for naught. For a while now, Teresa had been filled with spiritual longing. Her faith, which had once been so strong that she had even considered joining a religious order, was now so cold that she didn't even go to church anymore. She was searching for that "young woman who used to be her," the woman who had loved God so fervently. She now felt she wanted to reestablish that connection but wasn't sure how to begin. The moment she heard about the gift of one year, she knew exactly what her gift to herself was going to be. She would go to church every day, whether it was to go to Mass or just step inside a church for a few minutes to say a prayer. Teresa decided she was going to radically jumpstart a whole new relationship with God.

She started to plan her strategy. Teresa realized one important fact - if her plan was to succeed, it had to include flexibility. It might not be possible for her to go to mass every day, but visiting a church every day to pray was very possible. She would attend services when she could fit them into her schedule or find the time to enter a church just to pray. She made a commitment to visit a church each day for one year. She would sit quietly and converse intimately with God daily. She would have actual conversations with him. She would start off by praising and thanking him for all his blessings. She would tell him about her day, discuss any problems she was having, asking for his advice. She would renew her relationship with God, her Father.

As she was making her plans, she became enthusiastic and excited. She was overflowing with happiness at the prospect of spending time quietly with our Lord each day for one whole year. This was the most precious gift she could give to herself. As the days drew nearer for her to start this commitment, Teresa was filled with great joy. Her desire to once again become closer to our Lord was becoming a reality, and all it would take was the free time she was willing to share with him each day.

Restarting her relationship with God became most important to Teresa. Stopping in church every day would not threaten the fabric of Teresa's world. No one would be shaken by it. Most people wouldn't even notice that she was visiting a church every day. In fact, when Teresa's husband found out that she was attending mass, he wondered out of curiosity, but did not say anything about it. Yet, it brought about a radical change in the quality of her life. She started to read books that were classics, her music became more selective, her movies and TV choices had substance and meaning. In other words, she was not absorbing junk food into her brain, any longer. If the things she was listening to, watching or reading did not increase the moral fiber of her character, they were eliminated from her choices. As a result of this commitment, Teresa became a new creation.

Teresa has learned from her past mistakes that she has much to lose and nothing to gain if she lets anyone or anything interfere with her newly forged relationship with God. As Saint Paul tells us in Romans 8:38 she has learned "that neither death, nor life, nor angels, nor principalities, nor powers, nor things to come, nor any creature" shall separate her from the love of God. After many years Teresa still visits her Lord every day and she makes sure to guard her quality time with him. When she sits in church now, she remembers that young woman that used to be her, that young woman so filled with love and fervor for her Savior, and she thanks him for allowing her to be like that young woman once again.

If you decide to give yourself the gift of one year, start by asking yourself, "What do I want? How do I want to spend my free time for one year? How will I manage to find the time?" Before you start this venture, decide what it is you truly enjoy doing in your spare time. Then, in your daily routine, arrange to make time for yourself each day. Never feel guilty, or think that you are not worthy of the special time you have put aside for yourself. The gift of one year should make you feel better physically, psychologically, and spiritually. It should give you pleasure. It should not be time spent under pressure. The gift of free time should flow and feel natural. It should replenish you, and after the one year is over, I can guarantee that you will want to continue. In later years when you look back on your life, you will not regret that you did something you truly enjoyed, something you truly desired, something that made you feel that like the girl or boy that you used to be.

Here are some suggestions to help you give yourself the gift of one year:

1. Don't ask for time for yourself. Just take it. If you ask, people say "No." Don't feel guilty. If you take one hour a day for 365 days, it adds up to 365 hours for the year – a total of 15 days.

2. Explaining to others that you need time for yourself makes it more likely that you will get it. People will take your needs as seriously as you appear to take them.

3. Make appointments with yourself in your date book. When it's in your book in black and white, consider it sacred time.

4. Keep your appointments with yourself unless a dire emergency occurs.

5. Spend less time with people who waste your time. If you are besieged with time wasters, just ask yourself: "Am I getting anything out of the time I am spending with this person?"

6. Take an axe to the activities in your life that drain your time and aren't important. Less TV. Less shopping. Less house cleaning. Imagine yourself on your deathbed. If you will eventually regret having spent too much time doing these things, why do them now?

7. Whenever possible, say, "No" to unimportant tasks. Should people try to impose on you say you are sorry, but at this time you have a commitment to something you are doing for yourself, but don't get specific. Most times they are asking for things which are not important. We are not talking dire emergency here.

8. Set aside quiet time for yourself. An extra hour first thing in the morning, an extra hour at night can be the freest, quietest, most liberating time of the day.

Most women find it very difficult to put themselves at the top of the list. We set aside our own needs for those of others. If you keep in mind that giving yourself the time that you need will actually improve the quality of your relationships with those closest to you, it is easier to commit to allowing yourself the time. Anyone who has ever traveled on a plane knows that flight attendants instruct mothers, in the event of an emergency, to place an oxygen mask over their own face first, and their child's afterwards. A woman who does not care for herself will not be able to properly care for her loved ones. Give yourself the gift of one year; a gift to yourself; a gift to your loved ones; the gift of a lifetime!

Week Forty-Eight
Prayerful Reflection

Dear Lord,

You have created us and we are yours. We are the children of a generous and magnificent King and we want for nothing. We humbly kneel before your throne. Our only request is that you bless us with the discernment to know your holy will for us as we travel through this earthly life. Let your thoughts and words be ever in our hearts and on our lips. You are the good shepherd! We are yours and when you speak to us, we recognize your voice.

We wish to share the joy of knowing you with all those we meet. Help us to speak only what is pleasing and just in your sight. Grant us the gift to listen to others with whom we may not agree, but give us the courage not to follow those who would lead us into sin. Help us to be brave and speak up when there is an injustice. Help us to give aid to the downtrodden. Advise us when we should talk and when we are to be silent. Melt us and mold us into your image. Most of all fill us with your divine love so that we may see others with your eyes and your heart. Help us to obey your commandments. Also, give us the wisdom to understand that we must not live by the letter of the law, but by the law's spirit.

You have called us and we are yours. Lord, to whom else can we go? You alone have the words of eternal life, and our one desire is to dwell in your house all our days.

Week Forty-Nine
Inspired Thought

Now is the Acceptable Time

If I could save time in a bottle, the one thing that I'd like to do;
is to save every day 'til eternity passes away just spend them with you.
(Jim Croce)

Time, do we ever really understand how fleeting it is? Do we ever appreciate how precious it is? In 2 Corinthians 6:2-3, Saint Paul enlightens us: "Now is the acceptable time."

Many years ago, these were the words that came to me as I was helping a friend. Her mother had passed away, and she was doing the sad task of choosing the clothes she would dress her mother in while preparing for her funeral. She pulled open one of the drawers in her mother's bureau, and there, perfectly folded, lay beautiful slips, blouses, dresses and many other items of clothing, with their price tags still hanging from them. Her mother had never worn the clothes; she was saving them for a special occasion, for the acceptable time. My friend took what she needed from the drawer, gently closed it, and said, "Well, I guess this is her special occasion." She then looked at me with tears in her eyes and said, "Don't ever save anything for a special occasion. Every day of life is a special occasion."

I never forgot those words. We are living during a time when people accumulate so many belongings that they need to rent storage because there is not enough room in their homes to hold all of their possessions. Often times these items stay in storage until the person dies. The relatives then think of it as junk and discard it. In Luke 12:20, Jesus warns us against this in one of his parables. It is about a man who was storing his harvest in hopes of gaining a secure future for himself. God says to the man: "You fool! This very night your life shall be required of you. To whom will all this piled-up wealth of yours go?"

Avoiding accumulation of items we do not need or never use not only frees us, it presents an opportunity to share our excess with those in need. Eliminating possessions we will never use will help us make better use of all that we do possess. We must seize the day, remembering that each day is special and not put off using and enjoying our possessions, because tomorrow might never come. It is not yesterday, nor tomorrow, but now that is the acceptable time.

Week Forty-Nine
Prayerful Reflection

My Children,

The secret of life is not in getting more, but in wanting less. To simplify means not to deny yourselves the things you want, but to free yourselves from the things you don't want. The way to true happiness and peace is not to acquire more, but to find contentment in what you have.

Do not let your hearts be troubled when illness comes, when acts of betrayal occur, or when attacks from the evil one invade your lives.

I have authority over all that happens in the world. Do not be dismayed by the tribulations which are occurring. I know you find this hard to believe, but all things will be turned to the good, if you prevail. You may be surrounded by doom and many problems may confront you, but I have the power to deliver you safely from the foe. Put all your trust in me. That alone will make you feel secure and safe, and you will be anxious for nothing.

Enter my courts with thanksgiving. Let your requests and petitions be made known prayerfully, and my peace, which surpasses all comprehension, shall dwell in your hearts. By casting your cares on me, you will rest in me.

I have prepared this moment, this day, this year, and all of eternity just for you and we will rejoice in it. Again and again, I say that I want you to rejoice in my creation. It is my Holy Spirit that gives life. There is no profit in the things of the flesh. Heaven and Earth will pass away, but my words will not pass away.

Week Fifty
Inspired Thought

I Stepped into a Church One Day!

Part of my work is to suffer, and I am glad, for I am helping to finish up the remainder of Christ's sufferings for his body, the Church.
(Colossians 1:24)

I stepped into a church one day, knelt before the crucifix and prayed before the Blessed Sacrament... I was in pain. My back, knees, and every joint in my body were racked with pain. The right arm of Jesus lowered itself from the crucifix and his hand extended itself to me. I raised my right hand to take hold of his. Suddenly, it all became clear. The pain I was suffering was only a small portion of the pain he had endured to save me. I had the honor and privilege of kissing his hand in thanksgiving. He then raised his arm to where it had been, nailed to the crucifix. I left in gratitude, not noticing my own pain any longer.

I stepped into a church one day, knelt before the crucifix and prayed before the Blessed Sacrament...I was crying. I had lost someone very dear to me. I didn't know if I would be able to cope. I looked up at the crucifix. The eyes of Jesus were filled with tears. I felt their moistness as tears fell upon me. Suddenly, it all became clear. It was for my tears he died. He spoke to me: "Each time one of my children is abused, each time one of my children is lost, each time one of my children is damned because of their sinfulness, I too weep." I understood that I was not the only one who had to endure loss. His tears consoled me. I left in gratitude with the knowledge that this too, would pass.

I stepped into a church one day, knelt before the crucifix and prayed before the Blessed Sacrament...I was in despair. I had been betrayed. My heart was breaking. I would never be whole again. Rays of light penetrated my being as I knelt before him. He revealed his heart to me. It was surrounded by the slings and arrows that had been hurled at him during his trial, at his conviction, and finally at his crucifixion. All this he had suffered because of his love for me. Suddenly, it all became clear, "Why should it matter if others hurt and abuse me? He would never abandon me. I have his love, which is all that truly matters." I left in gratitude, knowing that without him, I have nothing and with him I have all I will ever need.

I stepped into a church one day, knelt before the crucifix and prayed before the Blessed Sacrament...I was filled with fear. I had just been diagnosed with leukemia and I was terrified. As I glanced at the crucifix, my eyes were drawn to his five wounds. He had shed his last drop of blood to save my soul. Suddenly, it all became clear. I realized that with him and through him and in him, his last drop of precious blood has the power to save my body, to restore my health, and to rekindle my spirit. I left in gratitude for the hope he had instilled me.

I stepped into a church one day, knelt before the crucifix and prayed before the Blessed Sacrament...I was filled with peace and joy! It was a perfect day and I was filled with happiness! I did not want for anything. I looked up at the crucifix. His eyes were fixed on me. They were filled with love and tenderness. His voice caressed: "You are my beloved child! Today you came before me, not asking, not requesting, and not petitioning. You came because you love me and wish to be in my presence. Always remember that the love you have for me is only a shadow of the love I have for you!" I left in gratitude, knowing that I am blessed to be so loved!

Week Fifty
Prayerful Reflection

My Children,

I am seated at the right hand of the Father, and hear all your prayers. You do not have to speak aloud. I see into the recesses of your heart; I see all that is hidden in secret. Learn to pray in earnest. Let your voice rise up to the heavens day and night. More things are wrought by prayer than this world can dream of. Your prayer should be the KEY of the day and the LOCK of the night. When you pray, it is more important to let your heart be without words than your words without heart.

I read your thoughts. You could never imagine how well I know you. I know every intimate detail of your life. I know your needs and will attend to each and every one of them mercifully. Call to me and I will answer you. I will show you great and mighty things; things of which you have no knowledge. Do not be astonished at the miracles that will occur in your daily life. Just come before me and surrender all that is worrying you. Learn to let go of all that is troubling you. My Spirit will instruct you as to the best solution for what is ailing you. Be still before me and know that I am your God. Look to me! I alone have the power to make good all that is disturbing your peace and happiness; but you must trust and believe that I can do what seems impossible to you. We are one and no one will ever snatch you from me. The works that I do in my Father's name testify to all I have told you. You are mine! I cherish you!

Week Fifty-One
Inspired Thought

The Blessed Sacrament

I am the bread of life. If anyone eats this bread he shall live forever.
(John 6:48)

We cannot visit our Blessed Lord too often. Our love of Jesus should then draw us to the tabernacle. There we shall find our supreme happiness at the foot of the altar; we shall find the courts of the Lord most attractive; we shall cry out with the prophets, "How lovely are thy tabernacles, O Lord of Hosts." But alas, how often the courts of the Lord are empty. The palaces of kings, princes and the rich are filled with visitors who pay them homage. Shall the palace of the King of Kings and Lord of Lords be deserted and forgotten? Although Jesus is always present in the tabernacle, he is infrequently visited. Jesus is there on the altar to welcome all, to bestow his grace on all, yet few come to visit him.

Taste and experience the sweetness of the love of Jesus in the tabernacle and spend some of the happiest moments of your life at his altar.

Blessed are they who dwell in thy house, O Lord. They shall praise thee forever and ever.

Week Fifty-One
Prayerful Reflection

Dear Lord,

In awe I humbly kneel before your throne. I clasp my hands in prayer. I offer myself to you in body and in soul. I only ask that you bless me with discernment to know your holy will for me. I wish to share the joy of knowing you with all those I meet. Let your thoughts and words be ever on my lips. Let me speak only what is pleasing and just in your sight. Advise me when I should talk and when I should be silent. Give me the gift to listen to others – even those with whom I may not always agree. Enlighten me to give aid to the broken and downtrodden. Give me the courage to speak up when there is injustice.

Melt me and mold me into your image. Help me to obey your commandments. Give me the wisdom to know that I must not live by the letter of the law, but by the law's spirit. Most of all fill me with your divine love so that I may see others with your eyes and your heart.

As I kneel here before you, I feel your presence in a very powerful way. You have called me and I am yours. Lord, to whom else can I go? You alone have the words of eternal life, and my one true desire is to live in your presence all of my days. I thank you and praise you for hearing my prayer. Amen!

Week Fifty-Two
Inspired Thought

His Eucharistic Presence

This is my Body to be given for you. This cup is the new covenant in my Blood which is shed for you. Do this in remembrance of me.
(Luke 22:19)

We who belong to the Catholic Church believe that the Blessed Sacrament is the true body and blood, soul and divinity of our Lord Jesus Christ under the appearance of bread and wine. Yes, we say we believe this beyond the shadow of a doubt, but all too often our belief is merely intellectual and we fail to think about the reality of our Lord's daily Eucharistic presence in the world.

There are many people who wish they had lived at the time of our Lord. Now it is two thousand years after the time Jesus walked the Earth in his visible humanity. At that time he was bodily present – in one place at a time and only a small number of people were blessed with the sight of his divine countenance. But now, in every place where the Eucharist is present, he himself truly abides. Consider this story:

"How is it possible," asked an educated Muslim "for Jesus to be wholly and entirely present in a little host?" The Bishop answered, "Look at the landscape before you and consider how much smaller the pupil of your eye is in comparison. This whole landscape can enter into your eye. If you can fit this enormous view into the pupil of your eye, cannot God, who can do all things, contain himself in the host?"

The Muslim then asked, "How is it now possible for the same Body of Christ to be present at the same time in all your churches and in all the consecrated hosts?" The Bishop answered, "Nothing is impossible with God and that answer should be sufficient, but nature also answers the question. Let us take a mirror. Throw it down on the floor and break it into pieces. Every piece can carry the same image that the whole mirror formerly reproduced. Likewise, the self-same Jesus reproduces himself, not as a mere likeness, but as a reality in every consecrated host. He is truly present in each one of them." Needless to say, there were no more questions.

Many of us live quite close to a church. Do we think of stopping in to visit him? Do we realize that he himself is there, as truly present as he was in the Holy Land twenty-one centuries ago? Do we realize that the same pierced hands are waiting there to bless us, the same gentle eyes to gaze upon us, and that the same tender heart is calling us, loving us, waiting for us to give him some little sign of love in return, or at least some sign of recognition – if nothing more than a genuflection?

Suppose you had lived twenty-one centuries ago, and by some happy chance had dwelt near the holy house at Nazareth. If our dear Lord had given you permission to come in and speak to him as often as you wished, would you not have found something to say? Would you not have wished to discuss with him every joy and sorrow you experienced in your life? Would you not have thanked him for gladdening the Earth with his presence, or acknowledged his kindness, or asked a blessing for yourself or others? Even supposing you had nothing to say, would you not still have loved to stay near him, blessed by the fact of his sacred presence?

Alas, people will cheerfully undergo endless pains and hardships in making pilgrimages to see holy relics and holy places, and yet they will not turn down the street in order to visit him from whom both relics and places derive their holiness.

Truly we have eyes, but we do not see; ears, but we do not hear; and minds; but we do not understand. When you are in grief, go to the altar and kneel at the feet of Jesus, for there you will find peace and consolation. When you are beset with worries, doubts and discouragement, go before the Blessed Sacrament, and sit in the silence of his presence, for there you will find comfort.

If we only learn to realize that the Blessed Sacrament is our God, what a sense of joy and protection would enter our lonely lives; God living here with me; God living here for me. We would haunt our altars in every circumstance, in every grief or trial that comes into our lives.

Instead, good pious Christians who are oppressed with sorrow shut themselves up for days. They would not act this way if they remembered the Lord is with them in the Blessed Sacrament. They would know that the mere sight of their tears is prayer enough to receive his attention! God the eternal is the same now as then. He never sees his children weeping in his presence without being moved to compassion.

Let us resolve, then, never to pass a church without entering it. Let us not begrudge our Lord a few moments. If we are pressed for time, let us still enter, if only to genuflect and hurry out again. Even if we do not say one word, what does that genuflection mean? It is in itself an act of faith because by that reverent bending of the knee, we acknowledge the divine presence. It is a sign of love, for surely if we were indifferent to his presence, we would not have troubled ourselves to come in and pay him homage.

Our love for Jesus should draw us to the Blessed Sacrament where we shall find the courts of the Lord most attractive and we shall cry out with the prophet, "How lovely are thy tabernacles, O Lord of Hosts. My soul longeth for the courts of the Lord." (Psalm 84:1)

Do not delay. Jesus is waiting!

Week Fifty-Two
Prayerful Reflection

Dear Father,

We come before you again to give praise and thanks for all the many blessings you have bestowed on us. We know we are unworthy so we stand before you sinful and sorrowful. But you have called us and we have been open enough to respond to your call. We are blessed because you have revealed yourself to us in a personal way. You have chosen us. Every moment of our lives, help us to be aware of your guiding presence in our lives.

Our prayer group was inspired by your Holy Spirit, and so we come to this meeting place with our brethren to worship you in word and song. Every week we are enlightened through scripture, hymns and sharing. The mystery of your word is revealed to us through your Holy

Spirit dwelling within us. Although our backgrounds and customs are different, when we appear before you on Wednesdays at 8:00, we are one. We celebrate our differences because, despite them, it is your Holy Spirit that binds us together as one body. We pray that you bless our prayer group. We ask this for a selfish reason. It is because we need the prayer group. The spiritual nourishment we receive every week encourages us to go forth and evangelize to others who do not know your word.

Tonight we strongly feel the presence of our guardian angels hovering over us - these heavenly creatures which you have given to each of us. They encourage us to do your holy will and to grow in love and grace. As we speak of their presence, a smile breaks forth on their faces because even though they do your bidding, it pleases them to be remembered.

Lord, continue to bless and protect us from the evil one. We pray that we will not be led into temptation. Teach us to be steadfast and loyal to your holy will and never to wander from the path of holiness.

We have been blessed by you to go forth and be a light in the darkness. We must pass through the narrow gate. It is painful to go through the eye of the needle. We know that in the days ahead, we may be called on to do just that. The cross we carry is never easy to bear, but it is still lighter than the chains from which we were freed. With you, in you and through you, all things are possible. The martyrs of old knew this truth.

Thank you, especially, for coming to us in your humanity as your beloved Son Jesus Christ, our Savior! He has called us to go forth and be a light in the darkness. Because of your Son Jesus, death has been swallowed up in victory. We are a resurrection people. We celebrate Easter as the day our Lord rose from the dead. Let us rejoice and be glad in it. Each and every day of our lives no matter what happens, no matter what hardships we must endure – let us rejoice in the Lord for all that he had done for us. Give praise and thanksgiving to him from whom all blessings flow. Amen!

Part VI. Appendix

1.

How to Say the Rosary

Using the crucifix, start with the sign of the cross and the Apostles' Creed. Then pray the *Our Father* on the large bead, the *Hail Mary* on each of the three small beads. (The three Hail Mary's are said for an increase in the three theological virtues, faith, hope and charity.) Then pray the *Glory Be* on the next bead.

You are now ready to begin the first decade of the Rosary. Choose a set of Mysteries from the following below. Think about the first Mystery while you pray the Our Father on the large bead, the Hail Mary on each of the ten small beads, and add the Glory Be at the end. The Fatima prayer may be added after the Glory Be. This is called a decade of the rosary. Think about the other four Mysteries while you pray each decade in the same way.

You can stop after any decade and pick it up later at the next decade. Your rosary has five decades, and the Mysteries come in groups of five. That's the usual amount for a day. But you can use all twenty Mysteries and go around the rosary four times, if you wish.

At the end of five or all fifteen decades, add the *Hail, Holy Queen.*

THE MYSTERIES OF THE ROSARY

The Joyful Mysteries
(Mondays and Thursdays; Sundays of Advent.)

1. ***The Annunciation***: Mary learns from the Angel Gabriel that God wishes her to be the mother of God and humbly accepts. (Luke 1:26-38) ***Spiritual Fruit: Humility***
2. ***The Visitation***: Mary goes to visit her cousin Elizabeth and is praised by her as "blessed among women." (Luke 1:39-56) ***Spiritual Fruit: Love of Neighbor***
3. ***The Nativity***: Mary gives birth to Jesus in the stable at Bethlehem. (Luke 2:1-20) ***Spiritual Fruit: Poverty of Spirit***
4. ***The Presentation***: Mary and Joseph present Jesus to His Heavenly Father in the Temple of Jerusalem forty days after His birth. (Luke 2:22-39) ***Spiritual Fruit: Purity of Mind and Body***
5. ***The Finding in the Temple***: After searching for three days, Mary and Joseph find the twelve-year-old Jesus sitting in the Temple discussing the law with the learned doctors. (Luke 2:42-52) ***Spiritual Fruit: Obedience***

The Sorrowful Mysteries
(Tuesdays and Fridays; Sundays of Lent.)

1. ***The Agony in the Garden***: The thought of our sins and His coming suffering causes the agonizing Savior to sweat blood (*hematidrosis*). (Luke 22:39-44) ***Spiritual Fruit: God's will be done***

2. ***The Scourging****:* Jesus is stripped and unmercifully scourged until His body is one mass of bloody wounds. (Matt. 27:26) ***Spiritual Fruit: Mortification of the Senses***

3. ***The Crowning with Thorns****:* Jesus' claim to kingship is ridiculed by putting a crown of thorns on His head and a reed in His hand. (Matt. 27:28- 31) ***Spiritual Fruit: Reign of Christ in Our Hearts***

4. ***The Carrying of the Cross****:* Jesus shoulders His own cross and carries it to the place of crucifixion while Mary follows Him sorrowing. (Luke 23:26- 32) ***Spiritual Fruit: Patient Bearing of Trials***

5. ***The Crucifixion****:* Jesus is nailed to the cross and dies after three hours of agony witnessed by His Mother. (Matt. 27:33-50) ***Spiritual Fruit: Pardoning of Injuries***

The Glorious Mysteries

(Sundays except during Advent and Lent; Wednesdays and Saturdays.)

1. ***The Resurrection****:* Jesus rises from the dead on Easter Sunday, glorious and immortal, as He has predicted. (Matt. 28:1-7) ***Spiritual Fruit: Faith***

2. ***The Ascension****:* Jesus ascends into Heaven forty days after His resurrection to sit at the right hand of God the Father. (Luke 24:50-51) ***Spiritual Fruit: Christian Hope***

3. ***The Descent of the Holy Spirit****:* Jesus sends the Holy Spirit in the form of fiery tongues on His Apostles and disciples. (Acts 2:2-4) ***Spiritual Fruit: Gifts of the Holy Spirit***

4. ***The Assumption****:* Mary, having completed the course of her earthly life, is assumed body and soul into heavenly glory. ***Spiritual Fruit: To Jesus through Mary***

5. <u>**The Coronation**</u>: Mary is crowned as Queen of heaven and earth, Queen of angels and saints. ***Spiritual Fruit: Grace of Final Perseverance***

The Luminous Mysteries
(Thursdays)

1. <u>**The Baptism in the Jordan**</u>: Jesus is baptized by John the Baptist and is filled with the Holy Spirit. ***Spiritual Fruit: Gratitude for the gift of Faith***
2. <u>**The Wedding at Cana**</u>: Jesus performs his first miracle at the bidding of his mother Mary by turning water into wine. ***Spiritual Fruit: Fidelity***
3. <u>**The Proclamation of the Kingdom**</u>: Jesus' words regarding the acquisition of the kingdom and the importance of striving to holiness. ***Spiritual Fruit: Desire for Holiness***
4. <u>**The Transfiguration**</u>: While praying on a mountain with Peter, James and John, Jesus becomes transfigured before them and the voice of the Father speaks to them saying, "This is my beloved Son, listen to him." ***Spiritual Fruit: Spiritual Courage***
5. <u>**The Institution of the Eucharist**</u>: Jesus shares the last supper with his apostles, initiating the Eucharistic supper which we still share today. <u>***Spiritual Fruit: Love of our Eucharistic Lord***</u>

Prayers of the Rosary

When the Rosary is said in a group, the most of the prayers are divided into two parts, of which one person, or part of the group, says the first, while the others respond with the second. The divisions are indicated below with an asterisk (*). Where no division is indicated, the entire prayer is recited by *all. (The sign of the cross is recited by all or by the leader alone, the others responding "Amen.")*

The Sign of the Cross

In the name of the Father, and of the Son, and of the Holy Spirit. Amen.

The Sign of the Cross is made with the right hand by touching the forehead at the word "Father," the chest at "Son," and the left and right shoulders at "Holy Spirit."

The Apostles' Creed

I believe in God the Father Almighty, Creator of heaven and earth; and in Jesus Christ, His only Son, our Lord; Who was conceived by the Holy Spirit, born of the Virgin Mary, suffered under Pontius Pilate, was crucified, died and was buried. He descended into hell; the third day He rose again from the dead; He ascended into heaven and sits at the right hand of God, the Father Almighty; from thence He shall come to judge the living and the dead. * I believe the Holy Spirit, the holy Catholic Church, the communion of saints, the forgiveness of sins, the resurrection of the body, and life everlasting. Amen.

Lord's Prayer (Our Father)

Our Father, Who art in heaven, hallowed by Thy name, Thy kingdom come; Thy will be done on earth as it is in heaven. * Give us this day our daily bread; and forgive us our trespasses, as we forgive those who trespass against us. And lead us not into temptation; but deliver us from evil. Amen.

Mary Moussot

Hail Mary

Hail, Mary, full of grace; the Lord is with thee; blessed art thou among women, and blessed is the fruit of thy womb, Jesus. * Holy Mary, Mother of God, pray for us sinners, now and at the hour of our death. Amen.

Glory be to the Father

Glory be to the Father, and to the Son, and to the Holy Spirit. * As it was in the beginning, is now, and ever shall be, world without end. Amen.

Fatima Prayer

O my Jesus, forgive us our sins, save us from the fires of hell, and lead all souls to heaven, especially those most in need of Thy mercy.

Hail, Holy Queen

Hail, holy Queen, Mother of mercy, our life, our sweetness and our hope. To thee do we cry, poor banished children of Eve. To thee to we send up our sighs, mourning and weeping in this valley of tears. Turn, then, most gracious advocate, thine eyes of mercy toward us, and after this, our exile, show unto us the blessed fruit of thy womb, Jesus. O clement, O loving, O sweet Virgin Mary.

V. Pray for us, O holy Mother of God.
R. That we may be made worthy of the promises of Christ.

The following prayer may be added after the "Hail, Holy Queen":

Let us pray. O God, Whose Only-Begotten Son, by His life, death and resurrection, has purchased for us the rewards of eternal life: grant, we beseech Thee, that by meditating upon these mysteries of the most holy Rosary of the Blessed Virgin Mary, we may imitate what they contain, and obtain what they promise, through the same Christ our Lord. Amen.

2.

Miracle Prayer

I dedicate this prayer to all the priests, brothers, sisters, deacons and lay people who have been a part of the St. Frances de Chantal Prayer Group all these many years. I was inspired to write this prayer one day while attending Mass. As I looked toward the altar, I noticed the priest appeared so worn and tired. My heart was filled with pity for his hard work and dedication, and I felt the need to pray not only for him, but for all the true servants of the Lord. I especially lift up Father Robert Grippo, our founder. He was and is an inspiration of holiness to us all. You have done well true and faithful servant of our Lord! The reward that awaits you is great!

Dear God,

For all the priests, brothers, sisters, deacons and lay people who serve you devotedly and who at times may be discouraged, disillusioned, and in despair, please reward them with a miracle! Lord, hear my prayer!

I do not ask this for myself, but for all those who have dedicated their lives to serving you. I ask this for all the priests who have truly followed your commandments in thought, word and deed. I ask this for brothers, sisters, deacons and those belonging to religious communities who have given of themselves without counting the cost.

O God, make a miracle! They are not asking for one. I am! They are so faithful and devoted to you. They know and understand how privileged they are to be serving you, and that there is no greater calling. They live by faith and not by sight. It would be such a wonderful and awesome gift to witness a miracle from you. It would lighten their burden. It would inspire and strengthen them for the mundane tasks they face each day. Just a little miracle! It would put new hope in their eyes – a new spring in their step. It would lift them up! It would energize their spirit!

Your servants are tired, Lord. It hurts me to see how unappreciated they are and how they are sometimes taken for granted. They carry their heavy burdens without complaining, but I notice how their shoulders stoop with trying to help those who are in dire need. They exhaust themselves trying to make life better for others. They do it because they love you and are following your commandment to, "Love one another as I have loved you."

The world is filled with temptation. It is hard in this day and age not to weaken, not to stray. Pleasures of the world are constantly attracting them, and yet they hold on, remain true. At times, it seems such a losing battle; yet they go on. How my heart goes out to them in their struggle to remain faithful.

Lord, make a miracle! Give them a sign! Show them a glimpse of heaven! You see Lord; I know the difference a miracle can make. I once felt the burden, the despair that life holds. If I have a spring in my step, the strength to accept, if I have learned not to take things too seriously and realize that I am not of this world, it is only because you made a miracle for me which is permanently engraved in my being. We are one, never to part. This miracle gave me inexplicable happiness that is always with me, no matter what the circumstances may be.

While you walked the Earth, you performed many miracles. Lord, is it too much for me to ask that you make a miracle now? O Lord, what a difference it would make in their lives. Father, I thank you for hearing my prayer asking you for a miracle. I know that you hear all my prayers, but I am asking for a miracle for all those who serve you so that they may continue to believe. Amen!

Author's Comment:

Pope Benedict XVI recently declared a Year of the Priest in an effort to encourage "spiritual perfection" in priests and to recognize the importance of the priesthood. The pope underlined the necessary and "indispensable struggle for moral perfection which must dwell in every authentically priestly heart." The pope will also proclaim St. John Vianney to be patron saint of all the world's priests. During this declaration, the Pope also emphasized that how, without priestly ministry, there would be no Eucharist, no mission and even no church.

I along with many others, feel that this is long overdue. It is heartening that Pope Benedict has not only emphasized the essential role of priests in the church and their value to our Catholic faith, but has recognized the daily struggles that they face in their vocation. I truly believe that this will have a beneficial impact on all the priests who loyally dedicate themselves to serving God and his people. This acknowledgement will also help people served by priests in parishes and missions throughout the world realize and appreciate the guidance and consolation that priests render to those that they serve.

I pray that this declaration of a Year of the Priest will not only help to strengthen those that already serve in this essential vocation, but that it will also inspire others to recognize that they are being called into the service of the Lord and his church. I am looking forward to this great celebration of the Year of the Priesthood! May God bless all of our priests, past, present and future!

3.

Baptism in the Holy Spirit
Inspired Thought

The Spirit and the bride say, "Come!"
And let everyone who hears say, "Come!"
And let everyone who is thirsty say, "Come!"
Let them all come and drink the water of life without charge.
(Revelations 22:17)

Once a year, all new members of the St. Frances de Chantal Prayer Group are invited to take a seminar called "Baptism in the Holy Spirit," which lasts approximately six weeks. Once the seminar is complete, there is special night of celebration where all the participants are prayed over. All members lay hands on one another, and scripture readings referring to the gifts and fruits of the Holy Spirit are spoken. We especially pray that the Holy Spirit fill the newly baptized with the gifts and fruits needed to boldly share the gospel with others. Experiencing the seminar and preparing oneself for Baptism in the

Holy Spirit is something that remains with you always. Anyone who has taken the seminar and been baptized will tell you the same thing.

It is just something you do not forget.

> *It is as though a seed has been planted in you; you are now pregnant. This pregnancy knows no race, color, creed or gender. It grows in both men and women. It is different from an ordinary pregnancy, yet it has something in common. It gives life. It is the basis, it is the root, and it is the foundation of your spiritual life. Just like any other pregnancy, it must be nurtured. This seed that is within you must be fed through prayer, scripture reading, attendance of mass, and reception of the Holy Eucharist. The more you sit at the feet of Jesus and become like Mary in choosing the better portion, the more the seed will grow.*

> *A power from on high will come upon you. You will be transformed and become aware of the fruits that are within you. The fruits of the Spirit are love, joy, peace, patient endurance, kindness, generosity, faith, mildness, and chastity. You will become a new creation. The Holy Spirit who is also known as the Consoler, the Advocate, and the Helper will fill you with gifts which will differ for each according to the favor bestowed from on high. One may have the gift of prophecy, another, the gift of ministry and service; another, the gift of teaching, another, the gift of tongues, and another, the gift of healing. These gifts are to be used to build up the Body of Christ.*

Jesus commanded the apostles to go forth and make disciples of all the nations. He filled them with the Holy Spirit to give them the courage to do this. Like the disciples, Jesus has commanded us to also go forth and make disciples of all nations. Like the disciples, we also need the empowerment of the Holy Spirit to do this. This is the purpose of

Baptism in the Holy Spirit – to give us the strength, courage, persistence and endurance necessary to proclaim the word and to reveal to the world what Jesus has done for us so that we can continue the work of the disciples to build up the Body of Christ.

Although we personally benefit from possessing the Holy Spirit, we receive a greater benefit when we allow the gifts of the Holy Spirit to flow through us to others. When we do this, we are using these gifts for the purpose they were intended, namely to spread the gospel. The Holy Spirit is a gift that is given freely to us and that we have accepted. It is a gift that is to be given graciously and accepted sincerely. It is our responsibility accept our gift sincerely and to share it graciously with others so that they in turn, can allow the gifts to flow through themselves to others. The gifts must flow through us in the same way as the flowing water of our baptism. It is living water, and we are living vessels that carry it.

Consider this: *In the land where Jesus walked, there are two bodies of water that are both fed by the fresh waters of the Jordan River. The larger is the Dead Sea. It is called this because nothing can live in its waters. The other is the Sea of Galilee. It is today as it was in the days of Jesus, a major source for the fishing industry. It holds what the Bible calls "living waters," water that is flowing and life giving. What is the difference between these two bodies of water? The difference is simply this; the Sea of Galilee has an outlet; it passes on the water as it receives it. The Dead Sea, on the other hand, holds onto every drop of water until it evaporates and leaves a bitter salt. It must have an outlet like the Sea of Galilee if it is to remain living water.*

Like the Sea of Galilee, we must pass on the gifts of Holy Spirit as we receive them to allow them to flow purely. Stagnant water is dead water, but flowing water is life sustaining. God is continuously giving the Holy Spirit to us. The gift of the Holy Spirit is like a constant waterfall, ever-flowing with fresh abundance like the Father's permanent embrace or kiss. If the Holy Spirit is the river of life that flows from God and the Lamb, if the Holy Spirit is constantly being breathed forth, then our participation in that gift must also be a ceaseless act of accepting God's gift of the Holy Spirit. But here is the catch: unless we share that gift, we lose it. Unless we let the Holy Spirit flow through the seabed of our heart, the living water will evaporate just as it does in the Dead Sea.

This is why people receiving Baptism in the Holy Spirit are urged to let praise flow from their tongues. The gift of tongues may not be the only sign that the Spirit has been received; but it makes sense that if we receive living water, we need to let it flow through us somehow, and one of the first effects of the Holy Spirit is to make us a vessel of praise. There are other outlets, of course: prophecy, healing, words of knowledge, wisdom, and the service gifts, especially outreach to the poor. The point is that we cannot just remain passive if God wants to activate us, and that is what he wants to do through the gifts of the Holy Spirit. The parable of the talents tells us that burying our gifts is disastrous, while using them brings multiple rewards. Jesus says, "To anyone who has, more will be given and he will grow rich; from anyone who has not, even what he has will be taken away." The meaning is simple – you have been gifted with a gift that will grow, if you use it. You must use it or lose it.

Other people are waiting to receive the gift you have received. Although God has personally given you the gift of the Holy Spirit, it was not just for you that the gift was given. He has others in mind, those who are thirsting for the life giving water, as you once were. Once we are baptized in the Holy Spirit, the flow must continue from those baptized into the desert of people who are thirsting for living water. This is what Christ commanded us to do and this is what we must do!

In Mark 16:15-16 we are told: "Go, therefore, and make disciples of all the nations. Baptize them in the name of the Father, and of the Son and of the Holy Spirit. Teach them to carry out everything I have commanded you to do. And know that I am with you always, until the end of the world."

In Joel 3:1 we are reminded: "And afterward, I will pour out my Spirit on all people. Your sons and daughters will prophesy, your old men will dream dreams, your young men will see visions. Even on my servants both, men and women, I will pour out my Spirit in those days."

For those members who are newly baptized, our prayer is that the Holy Spirit lights a fire within you and makes of you a new disciple. For us members who were previously baptized, we recommit ourselves to the Lord and ask for his strength and guidance to serve him and continue his work.

Baptism in the Holy Spirit
Prayerful Reflection

My Children,

Tonight, feel the power of the Holy Spirit within you. My Father is very generous and this night his grace is being poured out abundantly on all of you whom he loves very dearly. If you know how to give good gifts to your children, how much more will my Father in heaven give the gifts of the Holy Spirit to those who ask him? Do not be afraid to ask. Your gift has been especially chosen just for you. It has been yours since the beginning of time. It is waiting for you to claim it. Accept it!

It is not by accident you are here this night. You are the disciples I will use to encourage others to believe that I am the life and the resurrection, and he who has been raised up from the dead will give eternal life to all his children.

The Good News you have received from witnesses who came before you, you must now pass on to those who come after you. I send you forth as my disciples to share this truth with those who do not know me. Fear nothing and no one. The Counselor, the Spirit of Truth, whom the Father sends to each and every one of you will teach you the words you must speak. I am the vine and you are the branches and if you remain in me, you will succeed in all your endeavors. Live completely in my presence. If you abide by these words, you will be victorious; you cannot fail. I have told you all these things so that the joy I have and feel for you may be in you and your joy may be complete.

4.

The Holy Spirit Knows Me

Iwould like to share with you an experience that I had when I was in the eighth grade and preparing to enter high school.

It was the last week of school and the graduating students were all given half-days. As I started home, I found myself walking with Frieda, a classmate. We started talking about the high schools we would be attending and our hopes for the future. She expressed to me how she didn't enjoy half-days since her mother worked until three and she didn't like being alone in the apartment where she lived. I invited her to join me for lunch. I told her my mother wouldn't mind. She happily accepted. When we arrived home, my mother made us the good old standby, Campbell's soup and a tuna fish sandwich. She then announced that she was going to pick up a loaf of Italian bread, and said, "Enjoy your visit together!"

We were half-way through lunch when Frieda started to cry. I was flabbergasted and didn't know what to say. I thought I'd make light of it, and said to her, "Don't tell me the sandwich was that bad!" She explained to me that it wasn't the sandwich, but that she had a deep, dark secret that she had never told anyone. As she continued to cry, she asked me to promise that if she revealed the secret to me that I wouldn't tell anyone. I told her I wouldn't. She then blurted out the words, "I am illegitimate!" I didn't understand what those words meant. I was a very naïve girl of eleven and had never heard that phrase before. She then clarified by saying, "My mother and father were never married. I never knew my father. He ran away before I was born." I was truly shocked, because going back almost sixty-five years this was not a common occurrence. If you were born out of wedlock in those days, it was pretty serious. You weren't allowed to be baptized, or make communion and confirmation. I could see Frieda was truly upset and I didn't want her to feel worse, so I tried to appear nonchalant. I really didn't know what to say to make her feel better. As I look back, the next words I spoke proved to me that *I may not know the Holy Spirit, but the Holy Spirit knows me!*

I have no idea why I uttered the next words: "It's not so bad being illegitimate. Jesus was illegitimate, and he didn't turn out so bad." Frieda asked me to explain. I told her that I was required to take religious instruction before I made my communion and I remembered reading in the Gospels about Mary being pregnant with Jesus before she married Joseph. I told her that an angel had visited Mary and said, "The Son of God will be born to you by the Holy Spirit!" "So you see," I said, "maybe something like that happened to your mother." My words seemed to satisfy and comfort Frieda. We finished our lunch and before we knew it, it was time for Frieda to go home. The last few days of school, I didn't talk to Frieda again, except to wave hello to her in the hall.

The next time I was to meet Frieda, thirty-five years would pass. I was working for a senior citizen agency, and was the director of a "Meals on Wheels" program. It was one week before Christmas, and one of my co-workers asked if I would do her a big favor. She had ordered a doll from FAO Schwartz. They would not be able to deliver it before Christmas and so she asked if I could pick it up for her. I agreed to do it. I had never been in FAO Schwartz before, so I was quite impressed. It was like walking into a fairyland. I handed the saleslady the receipt and she went to retrieve the doll for me. As I was gazing at all the beautiful toys and displays, I heard a voice. "Mary, Mary Rossi. Is that you?" Someone was calling me by my maiden name. I looked up and around to see a beautifully dressed woman coming towards me. "I don't believe it, after all these years!" She gave me a big hug and I said, "Excuse me, but do I know you?" She started to laugh, "Mary, it's Frieda." I couldn't believe my ears. "Look," she said. "There's a coffee shop across the street. Finish your shopping and we'll have lunch together."

I picked up the doll and met Frieda in the coffee shop. She had already ordered soup and tuna fish sandwiches for both of us. "In remembrance of that day that I had lunch at your house," she said. "I never really thanked you. We were so young." "Frieda," I said, "no need for thanks, it was only a tuna sandwich." "No," Frieda said, "not for the sandwich, but for the comforting words you spoke to me that day." At that moment, I couldn't remember what I had said to her so many years ago. Frieda gave me a wink, and said, "Jesus was illegitimate! How did you ever come up with that one?" I replied, "If I knew that, I could pick tomorrow's lottery numbers." Frieda went on to say, "Mary, you don't understand the comfort that those words gave me. All my life, I was belittled by grandparents, aunts, and uncles telling me that I would never amount to anything, that I would grow up to be just like my mother, that I was sinful. You comparing me to Jesus and telling me that he hadn't turned out so bad, made me feel for the first time in my life that I was worthy and could amount to somebody important. Those words were just what I needed to hear at a time when I was very vulnerable. Thank you!"

Before we parted, Frieda gave me her phone number. I put it in the bag with the doll. When I reached the office, I handed my co-worker the package, completely forgetting the phone number was in the bag. When I finally realized my error, it was already too late. The bag had been discarded along with the slip of paper that Frieda had written her number on. All during our time together, Frieda and I never exchanged married names or addresses. There was no way we could get in touch with one another, and we have not seen each other since.

Not long after meeting Frieda, I joined the St. Frances de Chantal prayer group. It was then that I became aware of the Holy Spirit's presence in my life. Throughout the years, I have come to depend more and more on the power of the Holy Spirit to give me the words to speak when I am pressed to advise, console, or aid someone in distress, and I have never been disappointed. When I look back on that once-in-a-lifetime chance of meeting Frieda again, I realize it wasn't meant to rekindle a friendship, but to understand that those words of comfort that came out of me that day, came not from me, but from the Holy Spirit, speaking through me. These many years later, I realize that even when I was a very young girl, and thought that I did not "know" the Holy Spirit, the Holy Spirit always knew me. He knows us all!

5.

Members of One Body of the Church

A Chinese boy hurrying to the mission, unaware that it had been closed by the Communists, was stopped and questioned, "Where are you going?" The boy answered, "To catechism." "There is no more catechism," came the reply. "Then I am going to church," said the boy. "There is no more church," said the Communist. The boy answered, "I am baptized. I am the church!"

We are baptized. We are the church! We are all members of the Body of Christ. Saint Paul expresses it beautifully in 1 Corinthians 12:12-28:

> "Now, the body is not one member; it is many. If the foot should say, 'Because I am not a hand, I do not belong to the body,' would it then no longer belong to the body? If the ear should say, 'Because I am not an eye, I do not belong to the body,' would it then no longer belong to the body? If the body were all eye, what would happen to our hearing? If it were all ear,

what would happen to our smelling? As it is, God has set each member of the body in the place he wanted it to be. If all the members were alike, where would the body be? There are, indeed, many different members, but one body. The eye cannot say to the hand, 'I do not need you,' anymore than the head can say to the feet, 'I do not need you.' Even those members of the body which seem less important are in fact, indispensable. We must honor the members we consider less honorable by clothing them with greater care, thus bestowing on the lesser members an honor which the greater members already have. God has so constructed the body as to give greater honor to the lowly members that there may be no dissension in the body, but that all the members may be concerned for one another. If one member suffers, all the members suffer its pain; if one member is honored all the members share its joy. You then, are the Body of Christ. Every one of you is a member of this body. Furthermore, God has set up in the church first, apostles; second, prophets; third, teachers; then miracle workers; healers; assistants; administrators; and those who speak in tongues."

First and foremost, we are all members of the Body of Christ! The prayer groups that have sprung up since the Renewal are but an extension of his church. All of us who were part of the Renewal at its inception cannot convey to those who were not a part of this event how our lives were dramatically changed for the better. I owe a debt of gratitude to all the members of our prayer group and especially to those who have shared and witnessed to us every week for all these past years. Each member had their own individual gift which they shared with us. They were and are an inspiration to me and in thanksgiving, I dedicate this to them:

Wednesdays at Eight

In gratitude to those members of our Prayer Group who are:

The Head – The Core Ministry
But you, keep your head in all situations,
endure hardship, do the work of an evangelist,
discharge all the duties of your ministry.
(2 Timothy 4:5)

We receive our intelligence, wisdom and discernment from the brains with which God has blessed us. It is the head and brain that help the other members of the body to work in coordination with one another. Just as the body needs the head to keep its members in synch and working harmoniously together, so does our prayer group, need guidance, support and direction to function properly and harmoniously. Our Core Ministry serves us in this role. As Christ is the head of the church, so is our Core the head of our prayer group. Saint Paul tells us more about Christ's position as the head of the body of the church in Colossians 1:15-20:

> "Christ is the image of the invisible, the firstborn of all creation; for in Christ all things were created, in heaven and on Earth, visible and invisible, whether thrones or dominions or principalities or authorities—all things were created through Christ and for Christ. Christ is before all things, and in Christ all things hold together. *Christ is the head of the body, the church*; Christ is the beginning, the firstborn from the dead; that in everything Christ might be preeminent. For in Christ all the fullness of God was pleased to dwell, and through Christ all things are reconciled to God; whether on Earth or in heaven, making peace by the blood of Christ's cross. Jesus Christ is the center of creation, *the head of the church*, and both the human and divine One "in whom the fullness of God was pleased to dwell."

As it is that "in Christ all things hold together," so it is that because of our Core "all things hold together." Not only does our Core make us more cohesive, it makes sure that we place "Christ before all things" and that "all things are created through Christ and for Christ." The following prayer reminded me of the selfless manner in which the Core Ministry works to uplift our members, and by doing so, in turn uplifts our group as a whole.

Uplift
(By Father Maronic)

Let us be lifted up to you, O Lord.
Let us not see only ourselves, but help us to see you in others;
Let us not do only for the sake of doing,
but help us to unselfishly do for others.
Let our thoughts and actions be for those less fortunate than
   ourselves.
Let us rise above our own afflictions
and strive instead to see the pain and hurt in others.
Let us put as much joy as we can into the hearts of others.
Let us strive to lift up this fallen world by lifting up others,
   lifting them to the good and truth and beauty which is our
      birthright.
By thus lifting up others in a spirit of love and joy and service,
We will more surely be lifted up ourselves.

Our prayer group must always remain Christ-centered if it is to be successful and endure. To accomplish this requires not only intelligence and compassion, but high moral character as well. We are blessed to have a Core Ministry which is bestowed with all of these gifts. Their contribution to our prayer group's endurance is incalculable; they are beyond excellence. In their position as head of the prayer group, they serve not only with their heads, but with their hearts as well, and they are the cement which holds our group together. Paul's prayer in Ephesians 1:17-23 is my heartfelt prayer for the members of our Core Ministry:

"I pray that the God of our Lord Jesus Christ, the Father of glory, may give you a spirit of wisdom and revelation as you come to know him, so that, with the eyes of your heart enlightened, you may know what is the hope to which he has called you, what are the riches of his glorious inheritance among saints, and what is the immeasurable greatness of his power for us who believe, according to the working of his great power. God put this power to work in Christ when he raised him from the dead and seated him at his right hand in the heavenly places, far above all rule and authority and power and dominion; and above every name that is named, not only in this age but also in the age to come. And he has put all things under his feet and has made him the head over all things for the church, which is his body, the fullness of him who fills all in all."

In gratitude to the members of our Prayer Group who are:

The Arms – The Leaders
Like a shepherd he feeds his flock;
in his arms he gathers the lambs,
carrying them in his bosom, and leading them with care.
(Isaiah 40:11)

Arms are used to lift, support, embrace and lead. When we want to lead someone, or guide someone, or show them something, we take them by the arm. We walk arm-in-arm to support others, and to show affection for those that we care for. Some of our members are called to be leaders, the arms of our prayer group. Like our arms, genuine leadership supports, guides and uplifts people. Effective leadership does not alienate people; it involves them. It understands that people are more important than things, and that a leader is worthless and ineffective if he or she does not serve others as well as lead them.

At each meeting, a different leader is chosen to share and give witness to how the Lord has spoken to their heart. Every witness is unique because each leader imparts his or her own personality and character into it. A personal experience, an article from a book or newspaper, or a scripture passage shared by the leader with the group is the spark that inspires others present to share their own witness. We are blessed to have dedicated leaders who take the time to share their insights and testimonies of how God is present to them in a personal way. Our leaders use their words to lift our spirits, support us in our faith, and lead us to a closer relationship with God. This quotation from George Eliot reminded me of the relationship between our leaders and the other members of our prayer group:

> "O, the comfort, the inexpressible comfort of feeling safe with a person; having neither to weigh thoughts nor to measure words, but to pour them all out, just as they are, chaff and grain together, knowing that a faithful hand will take and sift them, keep what is worth keeping, and then, with the breath of kindness, blow the rest away."

In gratitude to the members of our Prayer Group who are:

The Eyes – The Youth Ministry
We are a people of faith and to have faith
is to believe what we do not see,
and the reward of this is to see what we believe.
(Saint Augustine)

The eye is the lamp of the body. When the eye is sound, the whole body is lighted and not in darkness. But as Saint Augustine is reminding us, just because our eyes work, it does not always mean that we "see". Perhaps this is why Jesus told us that unless we become like a little *child* we cannot *see* the kingdom of heaven.

> At the same time came the disciples unto Jesus, saying, who is the greatest in the kingdom of heaven? And Jesus called a little child unto him, and set him in the midst of them, and said, "Verily I say unto you: except ye be converted, and become as little children, ye shall not enter into the kingdom of heaven. Whosoever therefore shall humble himself as this little child, the same is greatest in the kingdom of heaven. And whoso shall receive one such little child in my name receiveth me." (Matthew 18:1-4)

It is the responsibility and duty of every parent to teach their children to become moral, compassionate and spiritually grounded human beings by their own example. But from an early age, children have much to teach us. Children are born as a clean slate, with none of the preconceived notions or baggage that adults carry with them. Children do not see color. They do not see hatred. They do not see bigotry. They only see these things if they are taught to.

<u>You Have To Be Carefully Taught</u>
(Oscar Hammerstein, 1949 "South Pacific")

You've got to be taught
To hate and fear
You've got to be taught
From year to year
It's got to be drummed
In your dear little ear
You've got to be carefully taught.

You've got to be taught to be afraid
Of people whose eyes are oddly made,
And people whose skin is a diff'rent shade,
You've got to be carefully taught.
You've got to be taught before it's too late,
Before you are six or seven or eight,
To hate all the people your relatives hate,
You've got to be carefully taught!

Through the years the young people that have joined us in prayer have taught us to see the world through unblemished eyes of acceptance, love, trust, joy and forgiveness. We are grateful for the youth that have joined us and taught us to how to stay not only young at heart, but young of mind and soul as well. Lord, may you always help us to see this earthly world and its creatures through the eyes of a child, so that we may someday be worthy to see your heavenly kingdom and dwell with you within it.

In gratitude to the members of our Prayer Group who are:

<u>The Holy Hearts – The Priests and Religious</u>
But thank God that, though you were once slaves of sin,
you became obedient from your hearts
to that form of teaching with which you were entrusted!
(Romans 6:17)

The heart is the center of our body. Without it, the others members would cease to function. But the heart is not only our physical center; it is our emotional center as well. There is something that is referred to as the "bible heart." From the different usages of the word, "heart," in the bible, it was determined that the heart consists of four elements: **emotion (to respond)**, will or **volition (to choose)**, the **intellect (to understand)**, and the **conscience (to discern)**. It is necessary for us to have and use each of these elements to become obedient to God's doctrine.

Through the years, we have had many priests, brothers, sisters, deacons, lay people, and people of other religious denominations join us on Wednesday nights to share and teach doctrine to us. What a blessing they have been to us! They have lifted our spirits with their sermons and inspired talks. They have supported us, encouraged us and taught us how to grow closer to God. Their holy hearts have touched us with their fire!

The Heart of a Holy Priest

A famous actor was at a gathering where he entertained the guests with stunning Shakespearean readings. As an encore, he accepted requests. A shy, gray-haired priest asked if he knew Psalm 23. The actor said, "Yes I do and I will give it on one condition: that when I am finished, you recite the same psalm." The priest, a little embarrassed, consented. The actor did a beautiful rendition, "The Lord is my shepherd; there is nothing I shall want..." When the actor was finished, the guests applauded loudly. Now it was the priest's turn. The priest stood up and quietly recited the same words as the actor. This time there was no applause, just a hushed silence and tears in the eyes of many of the guests. The actor savored the silence for a few moments and then stood up. "Ladies and gentlemen, I do hope you realized what happened here tonight. I knew the Psalm, but this priest knows the Shepherd."

The priests and religious that have been part of our prayer meetings have taught us that the heart is more than the physical, blood-pumping organ found in our chest. The heart involves the mind, will, emotions, and conscience of man. Their holy hearts have taught us and have done well in sharing with us "that form of teaching with which they were entrusted"!

A lawyer stood up to test Jesus. "Teacher," he said, "what must I do to inherit eternal life?" He said to him, "What is written in the law? What do you read there?" He answered, "You shall love the Lord your God with all your heart, and with all your soul, and with all your strength, and with all your mind; and your neighbor as yourself." And Jesus said to him, "You have given the right answer, do this, and you will live." (Luke 10:25-28)

Thank you to the holy hearts, the priests and religious who through their words and deeds have taught us to have hearts obedient to God's doctrine so that we too, might inherit eternal life.

In gratitude to the members of our Prayer Group who are:

The Voice – The Music Ministry
Praise him with the trumpet and harp.
Praise him with songs and dancing.
Praise him with stringed instruments and horns.
Praise him with loud clanging cymbals.
Let everything alive give praises to the Lord!
You praise him! Hallelujah!
(Psalms 150:3-6)

It would seem more than sufficient that when God created us he gave us the gift of speech so that we could express ourselves and communicate our thoughts and feelings to others using the spoken word. But the ability to use our voices to sing elevates the spoken word to a higher level, and is a gift that most fittingly is used to glorify he who bestowed it in the first place. Every

Wednesday we are reminded of this wondrous gift of voice and song that he has given us by "His Notes," our ministers of music.

How many times have we been comforted or inspired by a hymn sung by our Music Ministry? Seventy times seven? Nothing can lift one's spirit as much as an appropriate hymn sung in keeping with the theme of our meeting. Our ministers of music have not only enhanced our spiritual celebrations of the Mass and Baptism in the Spirit, but birthdays and special occasions as well. We are grateful for the many years our Music Ministry has inspired and entertained us with their special talents. Thank you to all the members of "His Notes," for elevating our prayer to a level more worthy of him through your gift of voice and song.

In gratitude to the members of our Prayer Group who are:

The Shoulders – The Male Members
I relieved his shoulder of the burden;
his hands were freed from the basket.
(Psalms 81:7)

Shoulders help us to carry our physical loads and also our emotional burdens. We cannot be on top of the world when we carry the world and its problems on our shoulders. Although pride sometimes prevents us from sharing our burdens with others, in our humanness, we must remember that we cannot do it alone and that at times we need to depend on others to help us through.

Many times women need the strength of a man to shoulder the burden of getting certain projects done. It is also comforting to have a man's broad shoulder to cry upon. Our male members are always ready to lend a strong shoulder to do both: to comfort and carry us through the emotional trials that we encounter and to help make easier many of the physical tasks that we are faced with. They use their strength to help us overcome our weaknesses, both spiritually and physically.

It is always nice to have a man around the house, and it is even better to have one around the prayer group. Our prayer group would be missing much if we did not have our male companions to accompany us as we praise and worship our Lord every Wednesday. We are grateful for the loyal and devoted male friends we have had through the years. May God continue to bless us with their presence, and the strength, comfort and relief that they so unselfishly provide to all those they encounter.

In gratitude to the members of our Prayer Group who are:

The Hallowed Hands – The Healing Ministry
He who labors as he prays lifts his heart to God with his hands.
(Bernard of Clairvaux – French Monk)

Hands are amazing instruments that allow us to do so many wonderful things. How appropriate then, that we are the work of the Father's hands. Hands, how marvelous you are! You are life itself! Hands enabled the evangelists to pen the words of the four gospels. The hands of Mozart played and composed magnificent masterpieces of music. A paintbrush in Michelangelo's hand resulted in the glory of the Sistine Chapel. Hands are God's co-workers. Jesus himself so often laid his hands on those in need of physical healing. Those same hands would later be nailed to the cross as the means to our spiritual healing. Thank God for hands!

Our healing ministers truly put their "hands to work and hearts to God," when they are called upon to stay after our meetings to pray over someone in distress. They lay hands on and lift hearts up in prayer to God to relieve physical, emotional or spiritual suffering. We have all experienced the comfort of someone's hand upon our shoulder or the relief provided by a loving hand stroking a fevered brow. How reassuring it is, when a comforting touch is coupled with such sincere, intense prayer. What dedication and devotion the members of our healing ministry have! When there are no words that will comfort or ease the touch of hands is most welcome to someone in crisis. We are truly blessed to have these ministers so willing to avail us of their gift of restorative prayer, which invokes the comfort and healing that can only be provided by a higher hand.

In gratitude to the members of our Prayer Group who are:

The Washers of Feet – The Hospitality Ministry
Then he poured water into a basin and began to wash his disciples' feet.
(John 13:5)

Although we are creatures created in the image of God, when our feet touch the Earth, we are reminded of our humanness. Feet remind us that we all stand on common ground; on the same Earth that God the Father created; the same Earth where his Son walked and dwelled among us.

Jesus used the feet to teach his disciples and us an important lesson. In John 13:13-15, Jesus explains the lesson to us and them in his own words:

> You call me Teacher and Lord, and you say well, for so I am. If I then, your Lord and Teacher, have washed your feet; you also ought to wash one another's feet. For I have given you an example, that you should do as I have done to you. Most assuredly, I say to you, a servant is not greater than his master; nor is he who is sent greater than he who sent him.

Christ humbled himself by washing the feet of his disciples. In doing so, he made it very clear that he would not expect anything from us that he was not willing to do himself. In doing this at the last supper, the night before he was going to die, Jesus left a lasting and important image for the disciples and all of us to remember: the importance of humbling ourselves in service to others. In following his example, our daily ministry to him must always begin at his feet in a posture of humility and absolute service before him and others.

Our Hospitality Ministry is an example of this. How can we ever repay them for the many hours they have spent serving us coffee and cake every Wednesday and preparing and arranging the food for all of our special occasions and celebrations? They come early, before the meeting, to set up and stay late after everyone has left to clean up and put everything away. How fortunate we are to have such willing and able angels to serve us so faithfully! The members of our Hospitality Ministry have humbled themselves as Christ did to serve others: tirelessly, faithfully, and willingly, week after week. Thank you for being Washers of Feet and reminding us to always serve others as Christ did by your unselfish example. Thank you, Ministers of Hospitality, from the bottom of our hearts, and our stomachs.

In closing, to each person I have ever encountered at one of our prayer meetings, I express these words of love:

> I thank my God every time I remember you. In all my prayers for all of you, I always pray with joy because of your partnership in the Gospel from the first day until now, being confident of this, that he who began this good work in you will carry it to completion until the day of Christ Jesus. (Philippians 1:3-6)

We are baptized. We are the Church. We are all members of the Body of Christ. Through our faith, through our gifts and through our service, we come together as a prayer group and miraculously become greater than the sum of our individual parts. It is only through God that this is possible. Therefore, we thank him and praise him for all of the abundant blessings which have come to us and anyone that has ever entered our church hall and joined our prayer group. May we always remember to thank him in every circumstance, and especially for every person who has ever walked through the portal of the St. Frances de Chantal Prayer Group, and graced us with their presence, Wednesdays at Eight.

With Appreciation and Thanks

To all my family and friends who said, "It's a good idea! Go for it! Thank you!

To my daughter Mary, for coming to my aid when I was having difficulty getting the computer to behave and for the hours she spent formatting the final draft. I couldn't have completed the book without her guidance. Thank you!

To my precious granddaughter, Mary Kate Mutze, an avid reader, whose suggestions and opinions concerning the format of the book were very much welcomed by the author. Thank you!

About the Author

As far back as she can remember Mary Moussot has delighted her family and friends by writing short stories about them. She is a born storyteller, and writing is pure pleasure for her. Mary lives in the Throgs Neck section of the Bronx. She and her husband Pete were married for 52 years before his death in 2007. Together, they became the proud parents of three sons and one daughter, and even prouder grandparents of six beautiful grandchildren.

This book captures Mary's experience as a member of the St. Frances de Chantal Charismatic Prayer Group which has met Wednesdays at Eight for nearly 30 years. It recounts not only the spiritual journey she shared with this special group but also her written inspirations. This work came into fruition because of her desire to share this journey and written inspirations with others.

Breinigsville, PA USA
07 December 2009

228793BV00001B/8/P